THE
NORTH AMERICAN

Maria Thun
BIODYNAMIC
ALMANAC
2022

CREATED BY
MARIA AND MATTHIAS THUN

Floris
Books

Floris Books is proud to be part of the international biodynamics movement. We aim to support biodynamic farmers, small-holders, wine-makers and gardeners by publishing informative and inspiring books, almanacs and apps.

Compiled by Titia and Friedrich Thun
Translated by Bernard Jarman
Additional astronomical material
by Wolfgang Held and Christian Maclean

Published in German under the title *Aussaattage*
English edition published by Floris Books

British Library CIP Data available
ISBN 978-178250-734-5
ISSN: 2052-577X
Printed in Poland through Hussar

 Floris Books supports sustainable forest management by printing this book on materials made from wood that comes from responsible sources and reclaimed material

MIX
Paper from responsible sources
FSC® C144789

Contents

Preface

Just after last year's almanac was printed, we heard that Matthias Thun unexpectedly passed away. A few months before I had visited Matthias and his children, Titia and Friedrich, as I often did. We had discussed a closer working together. We also looked through some rough layout drafts I brought of the English version you now have, and talked about how to make the almanac more easily understood by those who had little previous experience of using it.

Some things, like the tree sowing and cutting times, were only given as dates in the German almanac. But in English our readers are spread from New Zealand to Alaska, so we needed more precise times that could be used in time zones far in the east or west. Together we calculated the times that first appeared last year in the English edition.

After seeking and listening to feedback from our readers, we have completely redesigned this year's almanac, mainly to give more space to practical hints of what to do in the garden or on the farm each month. The introductory and background text has been rewritten to help readers understand the principles behind the almanac.

We hope that this helps and would be happy to hear suggestions from our readers.

Christian Maclean
Editor, Floris Books

What are the basic principles of the almanac?

The information in this guide is based on over sixty years of research by Maria Thun, who lived in central Germany and for over fifty years produced this annual almanac. After her death in 2012 her son Matthias continued the work, and it is now produced by her grandchildren, Titia and Friedrich.

The principle that underlies this guide is that the Moon has a significant influence over the Earth. Not only does it control the tides, but it influences all living organisms, including the way plants grow.

From our perspective on Earth, the Sun passes through twelve star constellations every year – the signs of the zodiac, from Aries to Pisces. The Moon also passes through these constellations, but because the Moon circles the Earth once a month, it passes through all twelve constellations about once every month.

Each constellation is associated with one of the four classical elements – earth, water, air or fire. And each of these elements affects a different part of a plant:

- the earth element affects the roots
- the water element affects the leaves
- the air element affects the flowers
- and the fire element affects the fruit and seed

It is easy to understand why: the roots are down in the earth, the leaves are full of water, the flowers' perfume is carried by the air, and fire (or warmth) is essential for fruit to ripen.

Through the course of many agricultural trials over several decades, Maria Thun showed that plants thrived, yields were increased, and harvested produce lasted longer if plants were tended at specific times, according to the part of the plant that the grower wanted to enhance. For example, carrots thrived if they were tended during root times, and apples thrived if they were tended during fruit times. This almanac gives you all the information you need to tend your plants at the best possible times, for the best possible outcomes.

The details of this almanac take into account all aspects of lunar and solar cycles, star constellations and the movement of planets. It is used every year by people all over the world to decide when to sow, plant and harvest fruit (including grapes for making biodynamic wine), vegetables, flowers and crops, as well as by beekeepers and people who make butter and cheese, since all of these are influenced by the movement of the Moon.

How do I use the almanac?

Different parts of a plant are cultivated for food or other uses. Plants can therefore be divided into four groups:

- Root plants, like carrots and potatoes
- Leaf plants like lettuce, spinach and the cabbage family, as well as herbs
- Flower plants, like broccoli and cauliflower, as well as ornamental flowers
- Fruit plants, like beans and tomatoes, as well as the obvious apples, oranges, grapes, and so on

There is a full list of types of plants on p. 66 so you can be confident about which type of plant you're growing.

The growth of all garden and farm plants and crops is enhanced when the plants are sown, transplanted, hoed, weeded, cut back and even harvested when the Moon is in a constellation that matches the plant type.

The twelve constellations are grouped into four different types, which correspond to the four types of time in this guide:

- Virgo (♍), Capricorn (♑), Taurus (♉)   Root
- Libra (♎), Aquarius (♒), Gemini (♊)   Flower
- Scorpio (♏), Pisces (♓), Cancer (♋)   Leaf
- Sagittarius (♐), Aries (♈), Leo (♌)   Fruit, seed

What's shown in the almanac?

The dates are listed down the left-hand column.

The hours are listed along the top, from 12 (midnight) to 12 (noon) and on to 12 (midnight again).

Transplanting Time (see p. 11)

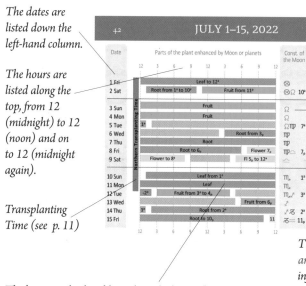

The column headed *Const. of the Moon* shows which star constellation the Moon is passing through, on that day.

The horizontal colored bars show the hours that are optimal for working on which type of plants. There are four types of time: *Root (brown bar), Flower (yellow bar), Leaf (green bar)* and *Fruit (red bar)*. There are also grey bars which are unfavourable times for working on any crop. (To find out why, skip ahead to 'Why are other astronomical events important' p. 12.)

The column headed *Solar and lunar events* shows other information about the Moon, Sun and sometimes other astronomical events (you'll find more about that in 'I'd like to understand the astronomy in more detail' p. 10).

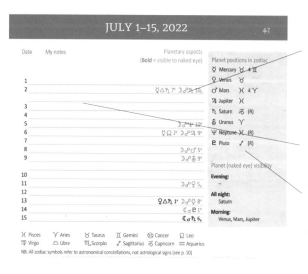

Planetary aspects and other astronomical information (see 'Why are other astronomical events important' p.12) are indicated on the right.

There is space for your own notes here.

The final (tinted) column shows which constellation the planets are in, and purely for those interested in astronomy, the naked-eye visibility of the planets (see 'Planets' p. 14).

Times and symbols

What time zone is the almanac in?

The times shown in this almanac are Eastern Standard Time (EST) or Eastern Daylight Time (EDT).

If you are not in that time zone, you'll need to subtract or add from the times in the charts according to your location (see page 17 'Converting to local times'). If you download the companion Biodynamic Gardening Calendar app, which uses data from this almanac and allows you to look up planting information while you're on the go, the app adjusts the times automatically to your location, but does not give as much detail as the printed almanac. (Details of the app are on the inside back cover).

Note that Fruit, Flower, Root and Leaf times normally don't last for precisely one day. The Moon moves in and out of different constellations at different times, so a Flower time might start at 11 am on a Monday and finish at 5 pm on a Wednesday. Use the colored bars to pinpoint whether conditions are favourable at a particular time on a particular day.

Do I need to understand all the symbols?

You do not need to understand all the astronomical background to grow better vegetables! If it is too daunting, just ignore it, and follow the practical hints for the type of plant you are growing at the times shown by the horizontal colored bars.

Why does the almanac recommend certain activities in the middle of the night?

Don't worry, no midnight planting is required! The almanac works for gardeners and farmers around the world, and one person's midnight is another person's morning or early evening. Just choose the times that work best for you. There are usually plenty of options for tending each type of plant.

Why does the almanac recommend that I harvest and store leaf plants during a Fruit and Flower times?

It may seem counter-intuitive, but it has been shown that Fruit and Flower times are best for harvesting and storing leaf plants such as lettuce, spinach and herbs.

I'd like to understand the astronomy in more detail
Star signs and constellations

The **zodiac** is a group of twelve constellations of stars, which the Sun, Moon and all the planets pass on their circuits as seen from the Earth. We know them as the zodiac – Scorpio, Cancer, Aries, etc. – but in the context of this guide, these names are used to indicate the visible star **constellations** rather than the astrological **signs** used in horoscopes. (For those who are into astronomy and astrology, the difference is that they are out of sync, as shown in the diagram below.)

The Moon takes about 27½ days to orbit the Earth, passing through all twelve constellations in that time. This rhythm is called the **sidereal month.**

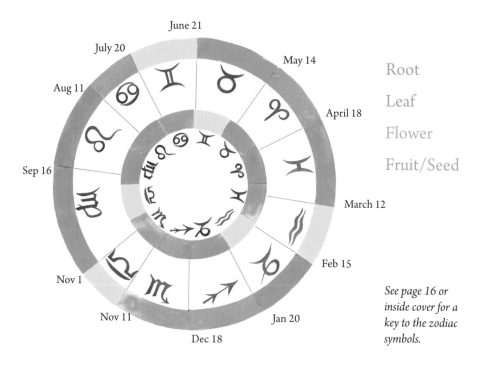

Root

Leaf

Flower

Fruit/Seed

See page 16 or inside cover for a key to the zodiac symbols.

*The outer circle shows the varying sizes of the visible **constellations** of the zodiac. The dates on this outer circle are the approximate dates on which the Sun enters the constellation (from year to year the actual date can change by one day because of leap years). The inner circle shows the divisions into equal sections of 30° corresponding to the **signs** used in astrology.*

Transplanting Time and ascending or descending Moon

From midwinter through to midsummer the Sun rises earlier and sets later each day, and its path across the sky ascends higher and higher. From midsummer until midwinter this is reversed: the days get shorter and the midday Sun shines from an ever-lower point in the sky. This annual ascending and descending of the Sun creates our seasons. In the northern hemisphere the winter solstice occurs in December when the Sun is in the constellation of Sagittarius, and the summer solstice occurs in June when the Sun is in Gemini. At any point from Sagittarius to Gemini, the Sun is ascending, while from Gemini to Sagittarius, it is descending. In the southern hemisphere, this is reversed.

The Moon (and all the planets) follow approximately the same path as the Sun around the zodiac but instead of taking a year, the Moon takes only about 27½ days to complete one cycle. This means that the Moon will ascend for about fourteen days, and then descend for about fourteen days.

When the Moon is *ascending,* plant sap rises more strongly. The upper part of the plant fills with sap and vitality. This is therefore a good time for cutting scions (young shoots for grafting). Fruit harvested during this period remains fresh for longer when stored.

When the Moon is *descending,* plants take root more readily and connect well with their new location. This period is referred to as the **Transplanting Time,** even though the period is actually optimal for a range of growing activities. Transplanting is when plants are moved from one location to another, for example when young plants are moved from the seedbed into their final growing position, but also when the gardener wishes to strengthen the root development of young fruit trees, shrubs or pot plants by frequently re-potting them. Note that sowing is the moment when a seed is put into the soil, and this can

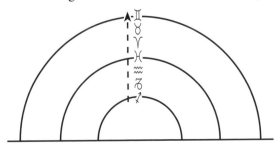

The northern hemisphere ascending Moon, showing the Moon's arc across the sky getting higher and higher for about 14 days, with the Moon moving from Sagittarius to Gemini.

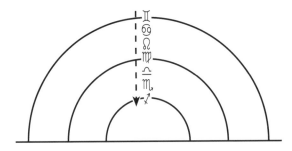

*The northern hemisphere descending Moon (**Transplanting Time**), showing the Moon's arc across the sky getting lower and lower for about 14 days, with the Moon moving from Gemini to Sagittarius.*

be done during either the ascending or descending period. We use the term 'transplanting' rather than just 'planting' to avoid confusion with sowing.

Additionally, because sap movement is slower during the descending Moon, it is a good time for trimming hedges, pruning trees and felling timber as well as applying compost to meadows, pastures and orchards.

You will sometimes see a reference to **Southern Transplanting Time**. This refers to the period of the descending Moon in the southern hemisphere, which is opposite to the time in the northern hemisphere.

In the 'Solar and lunar events' panel the date and time of highest Moon (⌢) is shown, after which the Moon descends, likewise lowest Moon (⌣) after which the Moon ascends. For the southern hemisphere these are the opposite way round: what is shown as highest Moon is the lowest Moon there.

One final note on the ascending and descending Moon: it is important to distinguish the journey of the Moon through the zodiac (sidereal rhythm) from the phases (waxing and waning); in any given constellation there may be a waxing or waning Moon.

Why are other astronomical events important?

There are many astronomical events in our skies, which also have an effect on the Earth, and this section gives more details about them and their effects.

They are important because some of them have an unfavourable effect on plant growth for some hours, and you shouldn't do any work in the garden during these times. These so-called *unfavourable times* are shown in the almanac as grey horizontal bars.

If you are not interested in astronomy, you can simply skip this section, but avoid doing anything in the garden during the times marked as unfavourable.

More Moon rhythms

The phases

The calendar pages show the phases of the Moon under 'Solar and lunar events'.

- ● New Moon
- ☽ Waxing half Moon (first quarter)
- ○ Full Moon
- ☾ Waning half Moon (last quarter)

This rhythm also takes about one month. Called the *synodic month,* it is a little longer – about 29½ days – than the sidereal rhythm that relates to movement through the constellations of the zodiac. This cycle does not have much effect on plant growth, and we take no account of it in this almanac; they are merely shown for those people who want to have a complete picture of the Moon's rhythms.

The Moon's nodes

The Moon's path through the zodiac is not exactly the same as the Sun's path (which is called the ecliptic). Seen from the Earth, the Moon's path is inclined by about 5° to the ecliptic. Twice a month, the Moon crosses the ecliptic, the Sun's path. These crossing points are called nodes. One crosses from below the ecliptic to above it and this is called the ascending node (shown as ☊ in the almanac under 'Solar and lunar events'). About two weeks later, it crosses from above to below; this is the descending node (shown as ☋). The times around the nodes are shown as unfavourable times (grey bars in the almanac). Both ascending and descending nodes have a negative effect on plant growth.

Eclipses

If a New Moon occurs at a node there is a solar eclipse, as the Moon is directly in front of the Sun. If a Full Moon occurs at a node there is a lunar eclipse, where the Earth's shadow falls on the Moon. Even if the eclipse is not visible from where you are, it has an unfavourable effect on plant growth and is shown as an unfavourable time in the almanac (grey bars).

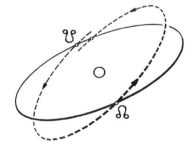

The Sun's path (solid line) and the Moon's path (dashed line) seen from the Earth (centre). The angle is exaggerated for clarity. The descending node (crossing point) is behind, and ascending node in front. (Note that the following node will not be in the same position: the nodes move.)

Apogee and perigee

The Moon travels on an almost circular ellipse around the Earth. This means that sometimes the Moon is a little closer to the Earth, and sometimes a little further away. The point at which the Moon is closest to the Earth is called perigee (shown as **Pg** under 'Solar and lunar events'). Conversely, the point at which the Moon is furthest from the Earth is called apogee (shown as **Ag**).

Perigee (**Pg**) is an unfavourable time (grey bars) for gardening work.

However, around apogee (**Ag**) the Moon stimulates flowering and fruiting. The almanac bars take account of this effect, which can mean that they diverge from the underlying Moon/constellation effect.

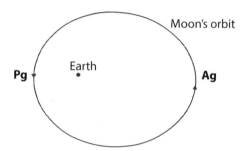

The elliptical orbit of the Moon around the Earth (exaggerated), showing closest (Perigee) and furthest (Apogee) positions.

The Sun and the zodiac

The Sun's movement through the zodiac takes a year and determines the seasons on Earth. The constellation through which the Sun is passing is always shown on the first entry of a calendar page, and if it changes during the month that is shown on the appropriate day. Remember that the almanac shows the visible astronomical constellations, and not the astrological signs, so the dates are out of sync! (See p. 10.)

Some activities depend on which constellation the Sun is in (for instance, making biodynamic preparations).

Planets

The planets, too, have an effect on plant growth. The far-right panel on the almanac pages shows which constellation each planet is passing. The planets mostly move in direct motion – that is, in the same direction as the Sun and Moon – but unlike the Moon, for some time they move in the opposite direction, which is called retrograde motion. (Retrograde motion can strengthen the effect of the planet.) This time is shown as R, with the date indicating when the retrograde motion begins. When the planet begins to move in direct motion again, it is shown as D.

The visibility of the planets to the naked eye is shown below this panel. This is purely an aid to personal observation and has no effect at all on farming or gardening! Note that the furthest planets, Neptune, Uranus and Pluto, cannot be seen with the naked eye.

Aspects

Aspects are particular angular relationships of planets, the Sun and the Moon (collectively called *celestial bodies*), as seen from the Earth. The main ones are *conjunctions*, which is when two celestial bodies pass each other; *oppositions*, which is when they are opposite each other; and *trines*, which is when they are 120° apart.

    ♂ conjunction   ♂° opposition   △ (or ▲) trine

For those interested in observing the planets, the aspects visible to the naked eye are shown in bold type.

Conjunctions

Conjunctions (shown as ♂) occur when two planets stand behind one another in space. Usually only the planet closest to the Earth has any influence on plant growth. If this influence is stronger than that of the Moon, cosmic disturbances can occur that irritate the plants and cause problems with growth.

This negative effect is increased if the Moon or Sun stand directly in front of a planet – called an *occultation* (●). In the case of Sun and Moon, this is called an eclipse. Sowing at these times will harm future growth and damage a plant's ability to reproduce. These times are marked as an unfavourable time (grey bar).

Oppositions

An opposition (shown as ♂°) occurs if two celestial bodies are opposite one another – 180° apart. You cannot see both planets during an opposition because one will be above the horizon, the other below. Their rays fall on to the Earth and positively stimulate the seeds sown at that moment. In trials, Maria Thun found that seedlings transplanted at times of opposition resulted in a slightly higher yield. While the opposition is shown under the planetary aspects, it is not otherwise noted on the calendar pages.

Trines

Trines (shown as △) occur when planets are 120° from one another. The two planets are usually both standing in the same type of constellation – Aries and Leo for example are both Fruit (fire or warmth) constellations. Generally, the positive effect of the trine overrules the underlying lunar constellation. There may therefore be a Fruit time shown in the almanac despite the Moon being in a Leaf (or other) constellation. To show that this is deliberate, there is a colored ▲ under 'Solar and lunar events'.

Sometimes when two planets are in a trine, they are in different types of constellations. The trine is shown as △ under planetary aspects on the right-hand page, but these trines have no effect on plant growth and are not shown as colored ▲ under 'Solar and lunar events' on the left page.'

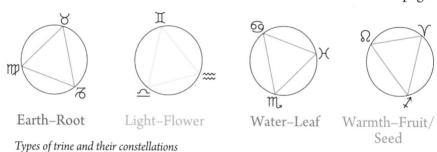

Earth–Root   Light–Flower   Water–Leaf   Warmth–Fruit/Seed

Types of trine and their constellations

Astronomical symbols

Constellations		Planets		Aspects	
♓	Pisces	☉	Sun	☊	Ascending node
♈	Aries	☽	Moon (first qtr)	☋	Descending node
♉	Taurus	☾	Moon (last qtr)	⌒	Highest Moon
♊	Gemini	☿	Mercury	⌣	Lowest Moon
♋	Cancer	♀	Venus	**Pg**	Perigee
♌	Leo	♂	Mars	**Ag**	Apogee
♍	Virgo	♃	Jupiter	☍	Opposition
♎	Libra	♄	Saturn	☌	Conjunction
♏	Scorpio	♅	Uranus	☀	Eclipse/occultation
♐	Sagittarius	♆	Neptune	☀	Lunar eclipse
♑	Capricorn	♇	Pluto	△	Trine (or ▲)
♒	Aquarius	○	Full Moon	D	Direct motion
		●	New Moon	R	Retrograde motion

Converting to local time

Times given are Eastern Standard Time (EST), or from March 13 to Nov 5 Eastern Daylight Saving Time (EDT), with ^{a} or $_p$ after the time for am and pm.

Noon is 12_p and midnight is 12^a; the context shows whether midnight at the beginning of the day or at the end is meant; where ambiguous (as for planetary aspects) the time has been adjusted by an hour for clarity.

For different time zones adjust as follows:

Newfoundland Standard Time: add $1\frac{1}{2}^h$
Atlantic Standard Time: add 1^h
Eastern Standard Time: do not adjust
Central Standard Time: subtract 1^h
  For Saskatchewan subtract 1^h, but subtract 2^h from March 13 to Nov 5 (no DST)
Mountain Standard Time: subtract 2^h
  For Arizona subtract 2^h, but subtract 3^h from March 13 to Nov 5 (no DST)
Pacific Standard Time: subtract 3^h
Alaska Standard Time: subtract 4^h
Hawaii Standard Time: subtract 5^h, but subtract 6^h from March 13 to Nov 5 (no DST)

Central & South America

Adjust as follows:

Argentina: add 2^h, but add 1^h from March 13 to Nov 5 (no DST)
Brazil (Brasilia): add 2^h, but add 1^h from March 13 to Nov 5 (no DST)
Chile: Jan 1 to March 12 add 2^h; March 13 to April 2 add 1^h; April 3 to Sep 3 do not adjust; Sep 3 to Nov 5 add 1^h; from Nov 6 add 2^h.
Columbia, Peru: do not adjust, but subtract 1^h from March 13 to Nov 5 (no DST).
Mexico (mostly CST): subtract 1^h, but from March 13 to April 2, and from Oct 30 to Nov 5 subtract 2^h

For other countries use *The Maria Thun Biodynamic Calendar* from Floris Books which carries all times in GMT, making it easier to convert to another country's local and daylight saving time.

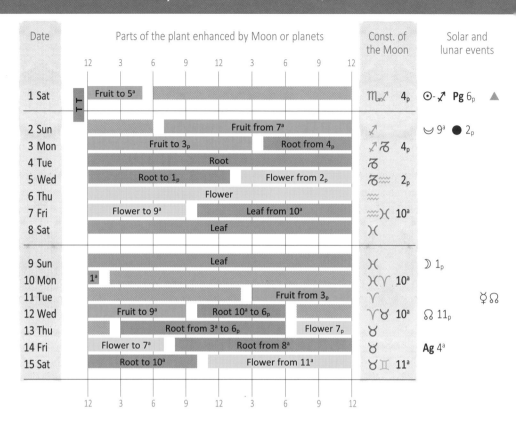

Date	Parts of the plant enhanced by Moon or planets	Const. of the Moon	Solar and lunar events
1 Sat	Fruit to 5ᵃ	♏︎ⰔⰎ♐ 4ₚ	☉-♐ **Pg** 6ₚ ▲
2 Sun	Fruit from 7ᵃ	♐	☽ 9ᵃ ● 2ₚ
3 Mon	Fruit to 3ₚ — Root from 4ₚ	♐♑ 4ₚ	
4 Tue	Root	♑	
5 Wed	Root to 1ₚ — Flower from 2ₚ	♑♒ 2ₚ	
6 Thu	Flower	♒	
7 Fri	Flower to 9ᵃ — Leaf from 10ᵃ	♒♓ 10ᵃ	
8 Sat	Leaf	♓	
9 Sun	Leaf	♓	☽ 1ₚ
10 Mon	1ᵃ	♓♈︎ 10ᵃ	
11 Tue	Fruit from 3ₚ	♈︎	☿ ♌
12 Wed	Fruit to 9ᵃ — Root 10ᵃ to 6ₚ	♈︎♉︎ 10ᵃ	♌ 11ₚ
13 Thu	Root from 3ᵃ to 6ₚ — Flower 7ₚ	♉︎	
14 Fri	Flower to 7ᵃ — Root from 8ᵃ	♉︎	**Ag** 4ᵃ
15 Sat	Root to 10ᵃ — Flower from 11ᵃ	♉︎♊︎ 11ᵃ	

Transplanting Time
(time of descending Moon in northern hemisphere)
Dec 20 to Jan 2 7ᵃ and Jan 16 7ᵃ to Jan 29 4ₚ

Fruit times
- Tend fruit plants (beans, grains, tomatoes) during these times.
- Plant bare-root fruit trees and soft fruit shrubs on unfrozen soil.

Leaf times
- Tend leafy plants (like lettuce) during these times.
- Sow winter lettuce and leeks in a greenhouse, or in warm regions in pots.

Flower times
- Tend flowering plants (broccoli, roses) during these times.
- Sow cauliflower in warm regions in pots.
- Plant flowering shrubs.

Root times
- Tend root plants (carrots, potatoes) during these times.
- Sow turnips in a greenhouse.

Date	My notes	Planetary aspects

Bold = visible to naked eye

$\odot \triangle \hat{\oplus}$ 5ᵃ

$\mathcal{D} \sigma ♀$ 5ᵃ $\mathcal{D} \sigma ♇$ 11ᵃ $\mathcal{D} \sigma ☿$ 10ₚ

$\mathcal{D} \sigma ♄$ 2ₚ

$\mathcal{D} \sigma ♃$ 10ₚ

$\mathcal{D} \sigma ♅$ 8ᵃ

$\odot \sigma ♀$ 8ₚ

$☿ \Omega$ 2ᵃ $\mathcal{D} \sigma \hat{\oplus}$ 7ᵃ

$\mathcal{D} \, {}^{\circ} \! \sigma^{7}$ 9ₚ

Planet positions in zodiac

☿	Mercury	♐ 1 ♑ (14 R)
♀	Venus	♐ (R)
♂	Mars	♏
♃	Jupiter	♒
♄	Saturn	♑
♅	Uranus	♈ (R)
♆	Neptune	♒
♇	Pluto	♐

Planet (naked eye) visibility

Evening:
Venus (to Jan 6), Jupiter, Saturn

All night: –

Morning:
Venus (from Jan 10), Mars

Pisces	♈ Aries	♉ Taurus	♊ Gemini	♋ Cancer	♌ Leo
Virgo	♎ Libra	♏ Scorpio	♐ Sagittarius	♑ Capricorn	♒ Aquarius

: All zodiac symbols refer to astronomical constellations, not astrological signs (see p. 10)

My notes

Southern hemisphere

Southern Transplanting Time
Jan 2 11ᵃ to Jan 16 3ᵃ and Jan 29 8ₚ to Feb 12

Milk processing

When **milk processing** it is best to avoid unfavorable times. This applies to both butter and cheese making. Milk which has been produced at Fruit times yields the highest butterfat content. This is also the case on days with a tendency for thunderstorms. Times of perigee (**Pg**) are almost always unfavorable for milk processing and even yoghurt will not turn out well. Starter cultures from such days decay rapidly and it is advisable to produce double the amount the day before. Milk loves Flower and Fruit times best of all. Leaf times are unsuitable.

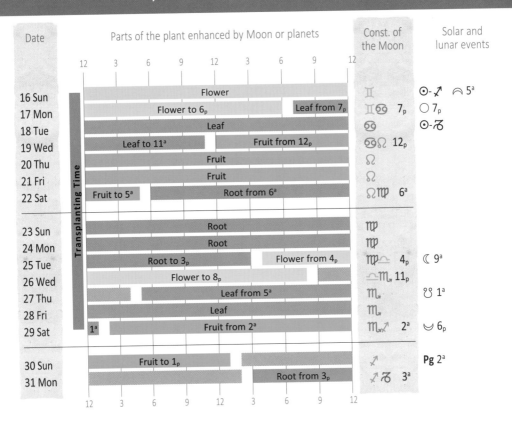

Date	Parts of the plant enhanced by Moon or planets	Const. of the Moon	Solar and lunar events
16 Sun	Flower	♊	☉-♐ ♈ 5ᵃ
17 Mon	Flower to 6ₚ / Leaf from 7ₚ	♊♋ 7ₚ	○ 7ₚ
18 Tue	Leaf	♋	☉-♑
19 Wed	Leaf to 11ᵃ / Fruit from 12ₚ	♋♌ 12ₚ	
20 Thu	Fruit	♌	
21 Fri	Fruit	♌	
22 Sat	Fruit to 5ᵃ / Root from 6ᵃ	♌♍ 6ᵃ	
23 Sun	Root	♍	
24 Mon	Root	♍	
25 Tue	Root to 3ₚ / Flower from 4ₚ	♍♎ 4ₚ	☾ 9ᵃ
26 Wed	Flower to 8ₚ	♎♏ 11ₚ	
27 Thu	Leaf from 5ᵃ	♏	☊ 1ᵃ
28 Fri	Leaf	♏	
29 Sat	1ᵃ / Fruit from 2ᵃ	♏♐ 2ᵃ	☋ 6ₚ
30 Sun	Fruit to 1ₚ	♐	Pg 2ᵃ
31 Mon	Root from 3ₚ	♐♑ 3ᵃ	

(Left margin: Transplanting Time)

Transplanting Time
(time of descending Moon in northern hemisphere)
Jan 16 7ᵃ to Jan 29 4ₚ

Leaf times
- Tend leafy plants (like lettuce) during these times.
- Sow lettuce and cabbage in greenhouse.

Root times
- Tend root plants (carrots, potatoes) during these times.
- In mild regions plant garlic.

Fruit times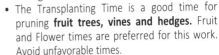
- Tend fruit plants (beans, grains, tomatoes) during these times.
- The Transplanting Time is a good time for pruning **fruit trees, vines and hedges.** Fruit and Flower times are preferred for this work. Avoid unfavorable times.
- In mild regions sow eggplant (aubergines) and chili peppers.

Flower times
- Tend flowering plants (broccoli, roses) during these times.
- Prune **vines, fruit trees and hedges** – see Fruit times above.
- In mild regions (or a greenhouse) sow begonias and cannas.

ate   My notes   Planetary aspects

(**Bold** = visible to naked eye)

	Planetary aspects
	$\odot_{\sigma}$ ♇ 10^a ☽$_{\sigma^o}$♀ 4$_p$
	☽$_{\sigma^o}$ ♇ 4$_p$
	☾$_{\sigma^o}$ ☿ 4$_p$
	☾$_{\sigma}$ ♄ 8^a
	☾$_{\sigma^o}$ ♃ 6$_p$
	☾$_{\sigma^o}$ ♆ 1^a
	$\odot_{\sigma}$ ☿ 5^a
	☾$_{\sigma^o}$ ♅ 6$_p$
	☿$_{\sigma}$ ♇ 11$_p$
	☾$_{\sigma}$♂ 10^a **☾$_{\sigma}$♀ 10$_p$**
	☾$_{\sigma}$ ☿ 9$_p$
	☾$_{\sigma}$ ♇ 1^a

Planet positions in zodiac

☿	Mercury	♐ 27 ♐	(R)
♀	Venus	♐	(R 29 D)
♂	Mars	♏ 22 ♐	
♃	Jupiter	♒	
♄	Saturn	♐	
♅	Uranus	♈	(R 18 D)
♆	Neptune	♒	
♇	Pluto	♐	

Planet (naked eye) visibility

Evening:
   Jupiter, Saturn (to Jan 21)

All night:
   –

Morning:
   Venus, Mars

Pisces	♈ Aries	♉ Taurus	♊ Gemini	♋ Cancer	♌ Leo
Virgo	♎ Libra	♏ Scorpio	♐ Sagittarius	♑ Capricorn	♒ Aquarius

My notes

Southern hemisphere

Southern Transplanting Time
Jan 2 to Jan 16 3^a and Jan 29 8$_p$ to Feb 12

My notes

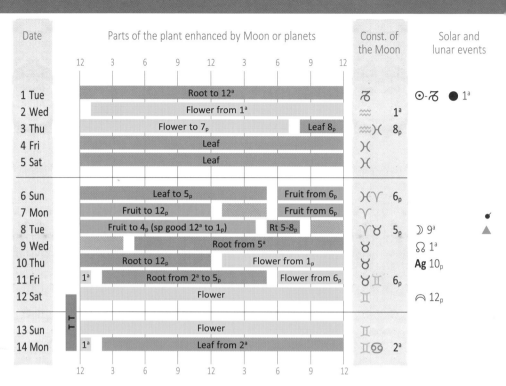

Date	Parts of the plant enhanced by Moon or planets	Const. of the Moon	Solar and lunar events
1 Tue	Root to 12ª	♑	☉-♑ ● 1ª
2 Wed	Flower from 1ª	♒ 1ª	
3 Thu	Flower to 7ₚ Leaf 8ₚ	♒♓ 8ₚ	
4 Fri	Leaf	♓	
5 Sat	Leaf	♓	
6 Sun	Leaf to 5ₚ Fruit from 6ₚ	♓♈ 6ₚ	
7 Mon	Fruit to 12ₚ Fruit from 6ₚ	♈	
8 Tue	Fruit to 4ₚ (sp good 12ª to 1ₚ) Rt 5-8ₚ	♈♉ 5ₚ	☽ 9ª ▲
9 Wed	Root from 5ª	♉	☊ 1ª
10 Thu	Root to 12ₚ Flower from 1ₚ	♉	**Ag** 10ₚ
11 Fri	1ª Root from 2ª to 5ₚ Flower from 6ₚ	♉♊ 6ₚ	
12 Sat	Flower	♊	◠ 12ₚ
13 Sun	Flower	♊	
14 Mon	1ª Leaf from 2ª	♊♋ 2ª	

Transplanting Time
(time of descending Moon in northern hemisphere)
Feb 12 2ₚ to Feb 25 11ₚ

Leaf times
- Tend leafy plants (like lettuce) during these times.
- Transplant lettuce and cabbage during Transplanting Time.

Root times
- Tend root plants (carrots, potatoes) during these times.

Fruit times

- Tend fruit plants (beans, grains, tomatoes) during these times.
- **Vines, fruit trees and shrubs** can be pruned during Transplanting Time from Feb 12 2ₚ selecting Flower and Fruit times as preference. Avoid unfavorable times.

Flower times

- Tend flowering plants (broccoli, roses) during these times.
- Prune **vines, fruit trees and shrubs** – see Fruit times above.
- Take **willow cuttings for hedges and fences** *outside* Transplanting Time (to Feb 12 10ª). In warm areas *during* Transplanting Time to avoid too strong a sap current.

ate	My notes	Planetary aspects

Planet positions in zodiac

☿ Mercury ♐ 13 ♑
(R 3 D)

♀ Venus ♐

♂ Mars ♐

♃ Jupiter ♒

♄ Saturn ♑

♅ Uranus ♈

♆ Neptune ♒ 8 ♓

♇ Pluto ♐

1 — ☽ ☌ ♄ 6ᵃ

2 — **☽ ☌ ♃ 7ₚ**

3 — ☽ ☌ ♆ 7ₚ

4 — ☉ ☌ ♄ 2ₚ

5 —

6 —

7 — ☽ • ♅ 3ₚ

8 — ♂ △ ♅ 10ᵃ

9 —

0 —

1 — ☿ ☌ ♇ 9ᵃ

2 — ☽ ☍ ♂ 11ₚ

3 — ☽ ☍ ♀ 1ᵃ

4 — ☽ ☍ ♇ 1ᵃ ☽ ☍ ☿ 5ᵃ

Planet (naked eye) visibility

Evening:
  Jupiter

All night: –

Morning:
  Mercury (from Feb 2),
  Venus, Mars

⧚ Pisces	♈ Aries	♉ Taurus	♊ Gemini	♋ Cancer	♌ Leo
♍ Virgo	♎ Libra	♏ Scorpio	♐ Sagittarius	♑ Capricorn	♒ Aquarius

B: All zodiac symbols refer to astronomical constellations, not astrological signs (see p. 10)

My notes

_____

_____

_____

_____

_____

_____

_____

_____

_____

_____

_____

_____

_____

_____

_____

Southern hemisphere

Southern Transplanting Time
Jan 29 to Feb 12 10ᵃ and Feb 26 4ᵃ to March 11

My notes

_____

_____

_____

_____

_____

_____

_____

_____

_____

_____

_____

_____

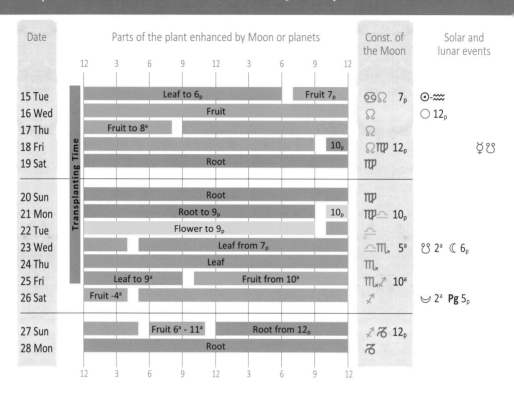

Date	Parts of the plant enhanced by Moon or planets	Const. of the Moon	Solar and lunar events
15 Tue	Leaf to 6ₚ — Fruit 7ₚ	♋♌ 7ₚ	☉-♒
16 Wed	Fruit	♌	○ 12ₚ
17 Thu	Fruit to 8ₐ	♌	
18 Fri	10ₚ	♌♍ 12ₚ	☿ ♊
19 Sat	Root	♍	
20 Sun	Root	♍	
21 Mon	Root to 9ₚ — 10ₚ	♍♎ 10ₚ	
22 Tue	Flower to 9ₚ	♎	
23 Wed	Leaf from 7ₚ	♎♏ 5ₐ	♊ 2ₐ ☾ 6ₚ
24 Thu	Leaf	♏	
25 Fri	Leaf to 9ₐ — Fruit from 10ₐ	♏♐ 10ₐ	
26 Sat	Fruit -4ₐ	♐	☽ 2ₐ **Pg 5ₚ**
27 Sun	Fruit 6ₐ - 11ₐ — Root from 12ₚ	♐♑ 12ₚ	
28 Mon	Root	♑	

(Left vertical label: Transplanting Time, spanning Feb 15–26)

Transplanting Time
(time of descending Moon in northern hemisphere)
Feb 12 to Feb 25 11ₚ

Leaf times
- Tend leafy plants (like lettuce) during these times.
- Transplant lettuce and cabbage during Transplanting Time.

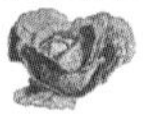

Root times
- Tend root plants (carrots, potatoes) during these times.
- Plant shallots and onions.

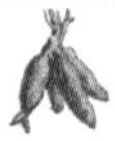

Fruit times
- Tend fruit plants (beans, grains, tomatoes) during these times.
- **Vines, fruit trees and shrubs** can be pruned during Transplanting Time (to Feb 25 11ₚ) selecting Flower and Fruit times as preference. Avoid unfavorable times.
- Sow tomatoes, eggplant (aubergines) and chili peppers in a greenhouse.

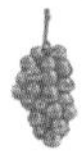

Flower times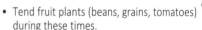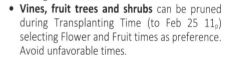
- Tend flowering plants (broccoli, roses) during these times.
- Prune **vines, fruit trees and shrubs** – see Fruit times above.
- Sow broccoli.
- Transplant any flower seedlings during Transplanting Time.

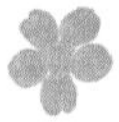

te	My notes	Planetary aspects

(Bold = visible to naked eye)

☽☍♄ 4ₚ — $\mathbb{D}\,\sigma^{\!o}\,\hbar\,4_p$

♀☌♂ 9ᵃ

☽☍♃ 12ₚ

☽☍♆ 8ᵃ   ☿☊ 9ᵃ

☽☍♅ 1ᵃ

☽☌♀ 4ᵃ   ☽☌♂ 5ᵃ   ☽☌♇ 10ᵃ

☽☌☿ 5ₚ   ☽☌♄ 9ₚ

Planet positions in zodiac

☿ Mercury	♑
♀ Venus	♐
♂ Mars	♐
♃ Jupiter	♒
♄ Saturn	♑
♅ Uranus	♈
♆ Neptune	♓
♇ Pluto	♐

Planet (naked eye) visibility

Evening:
Jupiter (to Feb 21)

All night: –

Morning:
Mercury (to Feb 25), Venus, Mars

| ♓ Pisces | ♈ Aries | ♉ Taurus | ♊ Gemini | ♋ Cancer | ♌ Leo |
| ♍ Virgo | ♎ Libra | ♏ Scorpio | ♐ Sagittarius | ♑ Capricorn | ♒ Aquarius |

B: All zodiac symbols refer to astronomical constellations, not astrological signs (see p. 10)

Beekeeping

Remove anti-bird nets and mouse guards to enable clearing flights.

My notes

Southern hemisphere

Southern Transplanting Time
Feb 26 4ᵃ to March 11

My notes

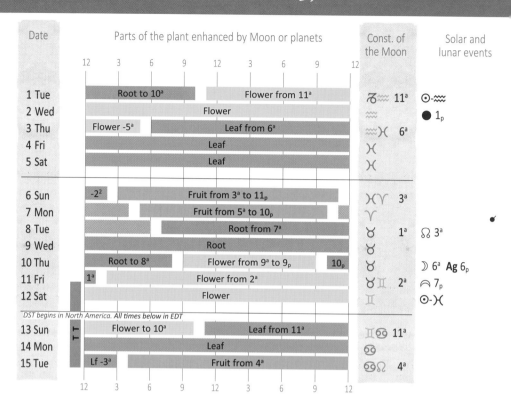

Date	Parts of the plant enhanced by Moon or planets	Const. of the Moon	Solar and lunar events
1 Tue	Root to 10ᵃ / Flower from 11ᵃ	♑♒ 11ᵃ	☉-♒
2 Wed	Flower	♒	● 1ₚ
3 Thu	Flower -5ᵃ / Leaf from 6ᵃ	♒♓ 6ᵃ	
4 Fri	Leaf	♓	
5 Sat	Leaf	♓	
6 Sun	-2² / Fruit from 3ᵃ to 11ₚ	♓♈ 3ᵃ	
7 Mon	Fruit from 5ᵃ to 10ₚ	♈	
8 Tue	Root from 7ᵃ	♉ 1ᵃ	☍ 3ᵃ
9 Wed	Root	♉	
10 Thu	Root to 8ᵃ / Flower from 9ᵃ to 9ₚ / 10ₚ	♉	☽ 6ᵃ **Ag** 6ₚ
11 Fri	1ᵃ / Flower from 2ᵃ	♉♊ 2ᵃ	⌢ 7ₚ
12 Sat	Flower	♊	☉-♓
DST begins in North America. All times below in EDT			
13 Sun	Flower to 10ᵃ / Leaf from 11ᵃ	♊♋ 11ᵃ	
14 Mon	Leaf	♋	
15 Tue	Lf -3ᵃ / Fruit from 4ᵃ	♋♌ 4ᵃ	

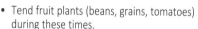

Transplanting Time
(time of descending Moon in northern hemisphere)

March 11 9ₚ to March 25 6ᵃ

Leaf times

- Tend leafy plants (like lettuce) during these times.
- Transplant spinach and lettuce.

Root times

- Tend root plants (carrots, potatoes) during these times.
- Sow carrots, radishes and turnips.
- Plant artichokes, horseradish and early potatoes.

Fruit times

- Tend fruit plants (beans, grains, tomatoes) during these times.
- Prune fruit trees and shrubs.
- **Cuttings for grafting:** cut outside Transplanting Time during ascending Moon. For fruit trees and shrubs, March 6 3ᵃ to March 7 10ₚ, avoiding unfavorable times.
- In warm areas plant cucumbers and tomatoes in pots.

Flower times

- Tend flowering plants (broccoli, roses) during these times.
- **Cuttings for grafting:** cut outside Transplanting Time during ascending Moon. For flowering shrubs, March 1 11ᵃ to March 3 5ᵃ and March 11 2ᵃ to 5ₚ.

ate	My notes	Planetary aspects

(Bold = visible to naked eye)

Planet positions in zodiac

☿ Mercury 7 ♒
♀ Venus ♐ 14 ♑
♂ Mars ♐ 4 ♑
♃ Jupiter ♒
♄ Saturn ♑
♅ Uranus ♈
♆ Neptune ♓
♇ Pluto ♐

Date	Aspects
1	
2	☿☌♄ 12ₚ ☽☌♃ 4ₚ
3	♂☌♇ 4ᵃ ☽☌♆ 7ᵃ ♀☌♇ 1ₚ
4	
5	☉☌♃ 9ᵃ
6	♀☌♂ 2ᵃ
7	☽●⚷ 2ᵃ
8	
9	
10	
11	
12	
13	☉☌♆ 8ᵃ ☽☍♇ 12ₚ
14	☽☍♂ 3ᵃ ☽☍♀ 6ᵃ
15	☽☍♄ 7ᵃ

Planet (naked eye) visibility

Evening:
–

All night:
–

Morning:
Venus, Mars

♓ Pisces	♈ Aries	♉ Taurus	♊ Gemini	♋ Cancer	♌ Leo
♍ Virgo	♎ Libra	♏ Scorpio	♐ Sagittarius	♑ Capricorn	♒ Aquarius

B: All zodiac symbols refer to astronomical constellations, not astrological signs (see p. 10)

Control pests
(see p. 74 for details)

Slugs: ash from March 13 11ᵃ to March 15 3ᵃ.

Southern hemisphere

Southern Transplanting Time
Feb 26 to March 11 5ₚ
and March 25 10ᵃ to April 8

Beekeeping

Willow cuttings for **pollen production** are best cut from March 11 9ₚ to March 13 10ᵃ; and for **honey flow** from March 15 4ᵃ to March 17 8ₚ. Avoid unfavorable times.

My notes

Biodynamic preparations

Pick dandelions in March or April in the mornings during Flower times. The flowers should not be quite open in the centre. Dry them on paper in the shade, not in bright sunlight. Once dried they can be stored until suitably encased and buried in the ground.

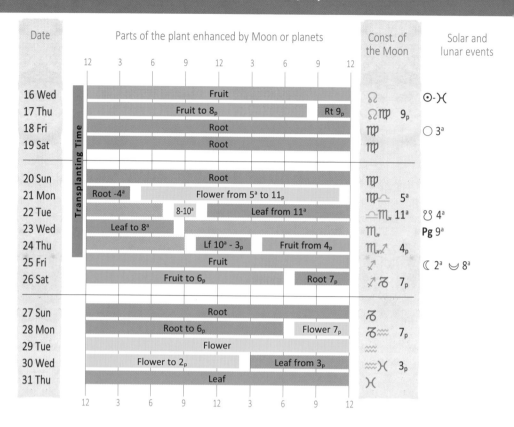

Date	Parts of the plant enhanced by Moon or planets	Const. of the Moon	Solar and lunar events
16 Wed	Fruit	♌	☉-)(
17 Thu	Fruit to 8p — Rt 9p	♌♍ 9p	
18 Fri	Root	♍	○ 3a
19 Sat	Root	♍	
20 Sun	Root	♍	
21 Mon	Root -4a — Flower from 5a to 11p	♍♎ 5a	
22 Tue	8-10a — Leaf from 11a	♎♏ 11a	☌ 4a
23 Wed	Leaf to 8a	♏	Pg 9a
24 Thu	Lf 10a - 3p — Fruit from 4p	♏♐ 4p	
25 Fri	Fruit	♐	☾ 2a ☽ 8a
26 Sat	Fruit to 6p — Root 7p	♐♑ 7p	
27 Sun	Root	♑	
28 Mon	Root to 6p — Flower 7p	♑♒ 7p	
29 Tue	Flower	♒	
30 Wed	Flower to 2p — Leaf from 3p	♒)(3p	
31 Thu	Leaf	)(	

Transplanting Time (vertical label, March 16–26)

Transplanting Time
(time of descending Moon in northern hemisphere)
March 11 to March 25 6a

Leaf times

- Tend leafy plants (like lettuce) during these times.
- Sow cabbage, Brussels sprouts, endives.

Root times

- Tend root plants during these times.
- Sow parsnips.
- Plant potatoes.

Beekeeping
Cut **willow cuttings** for **honey flow** from March 15 4a to March 17 8p. Avoid unfavorable times.

Fruit times

- Tend fruit plants (beans, grains, tomatoes) during these times.
- **Cuttings for grafting:** cut outside Transplanting Time during ascending Moon. For fruit trees and shrubs, March 25 10a to March 26 6p, avoiding unfavorable times.
- Sow melon seeds in pots.
- Plant strawberries

Flower times

- Tend flowering plants (broccoli, roses) during these times.
- **Cuttings for grafting:** cut outside Transplanting Time during ascending Moon. For flowering shrubs, March 28 7p to March 30 2p.

ate   My notes

Planetary aspects
(**Bold** = visible to naked eye)

Planet positions in zodiac

☿ Mercury ♒ 22 ♓
♀ Venus ♑
♂ Mars ♑
♃ Jupiter ♒
♄ Saturn ♑
♅ Uranus ♈
♆ Neptune ♓
♇ Pluto ♐

5   ☽ ☌ ☍ ☿ 10ₚ

7   ☽ ☍ ♃ 10ª   ☽ ☍ ♆ 7ₚ

8

9

0

1   ☿ ☌ ♃ 2ª   ☾ ☌ ♅ 9ª

2

3   ☿ ☌ ♆ 2ₚ

4

5

6   ☾ ☌ ♇ 6ₚ

Planet (naked eye) visibility

Evening:
  –

All night:
  –

7

8   ☾ ☌ ♂ 1ª   ☾ ☌ ♀ 10ª   ☾ ☌ ♄ 10ª   ♀ ☌ ♄ 4ₚ

9

0   ☾ ☌ ♃ 1ₚ   ☾ ☌ ♆ 6ₚ

1   ☾ ☌ ☿ 11ₚ

Morning:
  Venus, Mars,
  Saturn (from March 22)

♓ Pisces	♈ Aries	♉ Taurus	♊ Gemini	♋ Cancer	♌ Leo
♍ Virgo	♎ Libra	♏ Scorpio	♐ Sagittarius	♑ Capricorn	♒ Aquarius

Biodynamic preparations

Pick dandelions in March or April in the mornings during Flower times. The flowers should not be quite open in the centre. Dry them on paper in the shade, not in bright sunlight. Once dried they can be stored until suitably encased and buried in the ground.

Southern hemisphere

Southern Transplanting Time
March 25 10ª to April 8

My notes

My notes

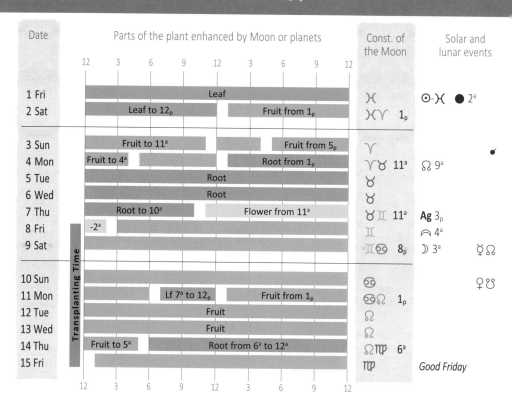

Date	Parts of the plant enhanced by Moon or planets	Const. of the Moon	Solar and lunar events
1 Fri	Leaf	♓	☉-♓ ● 2ᵃ
2 Sat	Leaf to 12ₚ / Fruit from 1ₚ	♓♈ 1ₚ	
3 Sun	Fruit to 11ᵃ / Fruit from 5ₚ	♈	
4 Mon	Fruit to 4ᵃ / Root from 1ₚ	♈♉ 11ᵃ	☊ 9ᵃ
5 Tue	Root	♉	
6 Wed	Root	♉	
7 Thu	Root to 10ᵃ / Flower from 11ᵃ	♉♊ 11ᵃ	**Ag** 3ₚ
8 Fri	-2ᵃ	♊	⌂ 4ᵃ
9 Sat		♊♋ 8ₚ	☽ 3ₚ ☿♌
10 Sun		♋	♀☋
11 Mon	Lf 7ᵃ to 12ₚ / Fruit from 1ₚ	♋♌ 1ₚ	
12 Tue	Fruit	♌	
13 Wed	Fruit	♌	
14 Thu	Fruit to 5ᵃ / Root from 6ᵃ to 12ᵃ	♌♍ 6ᵃ	
15 Fri		♍	*Good Friday*

Transplanting Time (vertical label, April 8 to 15)

Transplanting Time
(time of descending Moon in northern hemisphere)
April 8 6ᵃ to April 21 12ₚ

Fruit times

- Tend fruit plants (beans, grains, tomatoes) during these times.
- **Graft fruiting shrubs** outside Transplanting Times: April 2 1ₚ to April 4 6ᵃ, avoiding unfavorable times.
- Sow zucchini (courgettes) and squash.

Leaf times

- Tend leafy plants (like lettuce) during these times.
- Transplant endives, lettuce, cabbage, Brussels sprouts.

Flower times
- Tend flowering plants (broccoli, roses) during these times.
- **Graft flowering shrubs** outside Transplanting Times: April 7 11ᵃ to April 8 2ᵃ.
- Plant annuals and flowering shrubs.
- Prune flowering shrubs that have flowered.

Root times

- Tend root plants (carrots, potatoes) during these times.
- Sow turnips, rutabaga (swede).

Soil
The **soil warms up** on April 11.

te   My notes

Planetary aspects
(**Bold** = visible to naked eye)

☉☌☿ 7ₚ

☽•⊕ 2ₚ

♂☌♄ 10ₚ

☿☊ 3ᵃ ☽☍♇ 9ₚ

♀☋ 6ₚ

☽☍♄ 9ₚ

☽☍♂ 6ᵃ ♃☌♆ 11ᵃ

☽☍♀ 1ᵃ

☽☍♆ 6ᵃ ☽☍♃ 7ᵃ

Planet positions in zodiac

☿	Mercury	♓	10 ♈
♀	Venus	♑	2 ♒
♂	Mars	♑	10 ♒
♃	Jupiter	♒	2 ♓
♄	Saturn	♑	
⛢	Uranus	♈	
♆	Neptune	♓	
♇	Pluto	♐	

Planet (naked eye) visibility

Evening:
  Mercury (from April 13)

All night: –

Morning:
  Venus, Mars,
  Jupiter (from April 14),
  Saturn

Pisces	♈ Aries	♉ Taurus	♊ Gemini	♋ Cancer	♌ Leo
Virgo	♎ Libra	♏ Scorpio	♐ Sagittarius	♑ Capricorn	♒ Aquarius

: All zodiac symbols refer to astronomical constellations, not astrological signs (see p. 10)

Control pests
(see p. 74 for details)

- **Slugs:** ash from April 9 8ₚ to April 11 12ₚ.
- **Clothes and wax moths:** ash from March 30 3ₚ to April 2 12ₚ.

Good Friday and Easter

Maria Thun's research has shown that planting and other work is unfavorable from Good Friday to dawn on Easter Sunday, *local time.*

My notes

Southern hemisphere

Southern Transplanting Time
March 25 to April 8 2ᵃ and April 21 4ₚ to May 5

My notes

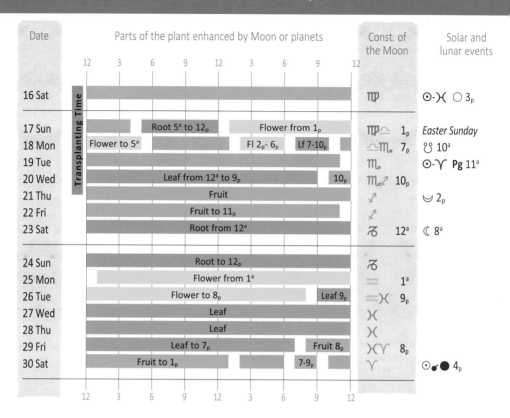

Date	Parts of the plant enhanced by Moon or planets	Const. of the Moon	Solar and lunar events
16 Sat	*Transplanting Time*	♍	☉-♓ ○ 3ₚ
17 Sun	Root 5ᵃ to 12ₚ — Flower from 1ₚ	♍♎ 1ₚ	*Easter Sunday*
18 Mon	Flower to 5ᵃ — Fl 2ₚ- 6ₚ — Lf 7-10ₚ	♎♏ 7ₚ	☋ 10ᵃ
19 Tue		♏	☉-♈ Pg 11ᵃ
20 Wed	Leaf from 12ᵃ to 9ₚ — 10ₚ	♏♐ 10ₚ	
21 Thu	Fruit	♐	☽ 2ₚ
22 Fri	Fruit to 11ₚ	♐	
23 Sat	Root from 12ᵃ	♑ 12ᵃ	☾ 8ᵃ
24 Sun	Root to 12ₚ	♑	
25 Mon	Flower from 1ᵃ	♒ 1ᵃ	
26 Tue	Flower to 8ₚ — Leaf 9ₚ	♒♓ 9ₚ	
27 Wed	Leaf	♓	
28 Thu	Leaf	♓	
29 Fri	Leaf to 7ₚ — Fruit 8ₚ	♓♈ 8ₚ	
30 Sat	Fruit to 1ₚ — 7-9ₚ	♈	☉ ☿ ● 4ₚ

Transplanting Time (time of descending Moon in northern hemisphere): April 8 to April 21 12ₚ

Leaf times
- Tend leafy plants (like lettuce) during these times.
- Mow lawns if you want to encourage vigorous growth of the grass.
- Transplant chicory, endives, cabbage, Brussels sprouts.

Root times
- Tend root plants (carrots, potatoes) during these times.
- Transplant **seed potatoes** for 2022 with Moon in Aries, from April 29 8ₚ to May 1 11ᵃ, avoiding unfavorable times.
- Sow salsify and parsnips.

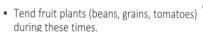

Fruit times
- Tend fruit plants (beans, grains, tomatoes) during these times.
- **Graft fruiting shrubs** outside Transplanting Times: April 21 4ₚ to April 22 11ₚ and April 29 8ₚ to May 1 11ᵃ, avoiding unfavorable times.
- Transplant eggplant (aubergines), tomatoes.

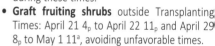

Flower times
- Tend flowering plants (broccoli, roses) during these times.
- **Graft flowering shrubs** outside Transplanting Times: April 25 1ᵃ to April 26 8ₚ.
- Transplant cauliflowers and broccoli.
- Plant begonias, dahlias, gladiolas and other annual flowers.

te My notes

Planetary aspects
(**Bold** = visible to naked eye)

☾☍☿ 7_p

☿☌⛢ 1^a ☾☍⛢ 7_p

☾☌♇ 1^a

☾☌♄ 8_p

☾☌♂ 9_p

☾☌♀ 1^a ☾☌♆ 2^a **☾☌♃ 7^a** ♀☌♆ 3_p

☿△♇ 8^a

♀☌♃ 5_p

Planet positions in zodiac

☿ Mercury	♈ 24 ♉	
♀ Venus	♒ 25 ♓	
♂ Mars	♒	
♃ Jupiter	♓	
♄ Saturn	♑	
⛢ Uranus	♈	
♆ Neptune	♓	
♇ Pluto	♐	(29 R)

Planet (naked eye) visibility

Evening:
Mercury

All night:
–

Morning:
Venus, Mars, Jupiter, Saturn

Pisces ♈ Aries ♉ Taurus ♊ Gemini ♋ Cancer ♌ Leo
Virgo ♎ Libra ♏ Scorpio ♐ Sagittarius ♑ Capricorn ♒ Aquarius

: All zodiac symbols refer to astronomical constellations, not astrological signs (see p. 10)

Control pests
(see p. 74 for details)

- **Clothes and wax moths:** ash from April 26 9_p to April 29 7_p.

Biodynamic preparations

Preparations can be taken out of the ground after April 18 avoiding unfavorable times (best at Fruit or Flower times). Preparations put into the ground after Sep 15, 2021 should wait until the end of May.

Good Friday and Easter

Maria Thun's research has shown that planting and other work is unfavorable from Good Friday to dawn on Easter Sunday, *local time.*

Southern hemisphere

Southern Transplanting Time
April 21 4_p to May 5

My notes

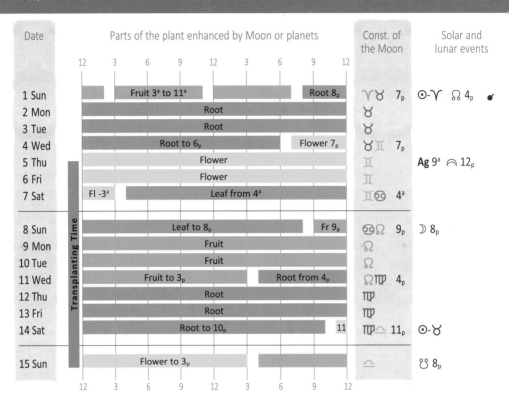

Date	Parts of the plant enhanced by Moon or planets	Const. of the Moon	Solar and lunar events
1 Sun	Fruit 3^a to 11^a; Root 8_p	♈♉ 7_p	☉-♈ ☊ 4_p ●
2 Mon	Root	♉	
3 Tue	Root	♉	
4 Wed	Root to 6_p; Flower 7_p	♉♊ 7_p	
5 Thu	Flower	♊	Ag 9^a ⋒ 12_p
6 Fri	Flower	♊	
7 Sat	Fl -3^a; Leaf from 4^a	♊♋ 4^a	
8 Sun	Leaf to 8_p; Fr 9_p	♋♌ 9_p	☽ 8_p
9 Mon	Fruit	♌	
10 Tue	Fruit	♌	
11 Wed	Fruit to 3_p; Root from 4_p	♌♍ 4_p	
12 Thu	Root	♍	
13 Fri	Root	♍	
14 Sat	Root to 10_p; 11	♍♎ 11_p	☉-♉
15 Sun	Flower to 3_p	♎	☋ 8_p

Transplanting Time (May 5 – May 15)

Transplanting Time
(time of descending Moon in northern hemisphere)

May 5 2_p to May 18 7_p

Leaf times

- Tend leafy plants (like lettuce) during these times.
- Plant aromatic herbs.
- Transplant cabbage.
- Sow lettuce, endives, parsley, chervil, kale.

Root times

- Tend root plants (carrots, potatoes) during these times.
- Transplant **table potatoes.**
- Transplant **seed potatoes** for 2022 with Moon in Aries, from April 29 8_p to May 1 11^a, avoiding unfavorable times.
- Sow beets (beetroots) and carrots.

Fruit times

- Tend fruit plants (beans, grains, tomatoes) during these times.
- **Graft fruiting shrubs** outside Transplanting Times: April 29 8_p to May 1 11^a, avoiding unfavorable times.
- Sow beans, zucchini (courgettes), cucumbers.

Flower times

- Tend flowering plants (broccoli, roses) during these times.
- Cut **hay** between May 4 7_p and May 7 3^a, and at other Flower times.
- Sow cauliflower and broccoli.

Beekeeping

Begin **queen bee** rearing (grafting or larval transfer, comb insertion, cell punching) between May 4 7_p and May 7 3^a and at other Flower times.

te My notes

Planetary aspects
(**Bold** = visible to naked eye)

Planetary aspects
☽☌♅ 1ᵃ
☽☌☿ 11ᵃ
☉☌♅ 3ᵃ
☽☍♇ 5ᵃ
☽☍♄ 9ᵃ
☽☍♂ 8ᵃ ☽☍♆ 5ₚ
☽☍♃ 3ᵃ
☽☍♀ 1ᵃ
☽☍♅ 8ᵃ

Planet positions in zodiac

☿ Mercury	♉	(10 R)
♀ Venus	♓	
♂ Mars	♒	13 ♓
♃ Jupiter	♓	
♄ Saturn	♑	
♅ Uranus	♈	
♆ Neptune	♓	
♇ Pluto	♐	(R)

Planet (naked eye) visibility

Evening:
Mercury (to May 11)

All night:
–

Morning:
Venus, Mars, Jupiter, Saturn

Pisces ♈ Aries ♉ Taurus ♊ Gemini ♋ Cancer ♌ Leo
Virgo ♎ Libra ♏ Scorpio ♐ Sagittarius ♑ Capricorn ♒ Aquarius

: All zodiac symbols refer to astronomical constellations, not astrological signs (see p. 10)

Control pests
(see p. 74 for details)

- **Flies:** burn fly papers in the cow barn at Flower times.
- **Chitinous insects, wheat weevil, Colorado beetle and varroa:** ash from May 1 7ₚ to May 4 6ₚ.

My notes

Southern hemisphere

Southern Transplanting Time
April 21 to May 5 10ᵃ and May 18 11ₚ to June 1

My notes

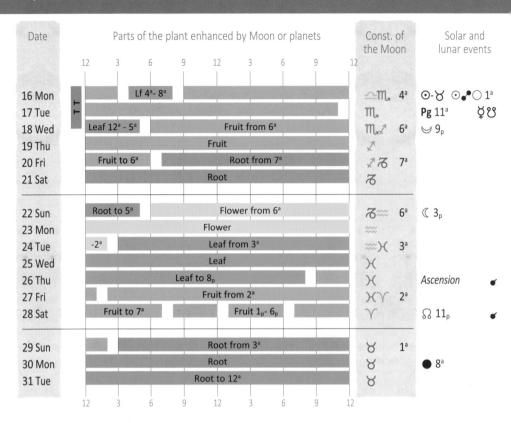

Date	Parts of the plant enhanced by Moon or planets	Const. of the Moon	Solar and lunar events
16 Mon	Lf 4ᵃ- 8ᵃ	♎ ♏ 4ᵃ	☉-♉ ☉•● ○ 1ᵃ
17 Tue		♏	Pg 11ᵃ ☿♊
18 Wed	Leaf 12ᵃ - 5ᵃ / Fruit from 6ᵃ	♏ ♐ 6ᵃ	☽ 9ₚ
19 Thu	Fruit	♐	
20 Fri	Fruit to 6ᵃ / Root from 7ᵃ	♐ ♑ 7ᵃ	
21 Sat	Root	♑	
22 Sun	Root to 5ᵃ / Flower from 6ᵃ	♑ ♒ 6ᵃ	☾ 3ₚ
23 Mon	Flower	♒	
24 Tue	-2ᵃ / Leaf from 3ᵃ	♒ ♓ 3ᵃ	
25 Wed	Leaf	♓	
26 Thu	Leaf to 8ₚ	♓	*Ascension*
27 Fri	Fruit from 2ᵃ	♓ ♈ 2ᵃ	
28 Sat	Fruit to 7ᵃ / Fruit 1ₚ- 6ₚ	♈	☊ 11ₚ
29 Sun	Root from 3ᵃ	♉ 1ᵃ	
30 Mon	Root	♉	● 8ᵃ
31 Tue	Root to 12ᵃ	♉	

(time scale: 12 3 6 9 12 3 6 9 12)

Transplanting Time
(time of descending Moon in northern hemisphere)
May 5 to May 18 7ₚ

Leaf times

- Tend leafy plants (like lettuce) during these times.
- Prune hedges.
- Transplant Brussels sprouts, celery, lettuce.
- Thin lettuce and chard.

Root times

- Tend root plants (carrots, potatoes) during these times.
- Transplant **table potatoes**.
- Transplant **seed potatoes** for 2022 from May 27 2ᵃ to May 28 6ₚ, avoiding unfavorable times.
- Sow winter radishes and carrots.

Fruit times
- Tend fruit plants (beans, grains, tomatoes) during these times.
- Prune suckers off tomatoes, cucumbers.
- Prune fruit trees after the fruit falls off.

Flower times
- Tend flowering plants (broccoli, roses) during these times.
- Cut **hay** between May 22 6ᵃ and May 24 2ᵃ, and at other Flower times.
- Layer climbing roses, clematis, honeysuckle.

Beekeeping

- Begin **queen bee** rearing (grafting or larval transfer, comb insertion, cell punching) at Flower times.
- Make and sprinkle **varroa ash** between May 29 1ᵃ and May 31 11ₚ.

te   My notes

Planetary aspects
(**Bold** = visible to naked eye)

$\mathbb{C} \, \sigma^{\!o} \, \Diamond \, 1_p$
$\Diamond \, \delta \, 9^a$
$\sigma^{\!} \, \sigma \, \Psi \, 3^a$
$\odot \, \triangle \, \mathrm{P} \, 8^a$
$\mathbb{C} \, \sigma \, \mathrm{P} \, 6^a$
$\odot \, \sigma \, \Diamond \, 3_p$

$\mathbb{C} \, \sigma \, \hbar \, 3^a$

$\mathbb{C} \, \sigma \, \Psi \, 9^a$ $\mathbb{C} \, \sigma \, \sigma^{\!} \, 6_p$ $\mathbb{C} \, \sigma \, \mathrm{2\!\!\!I} \, 10_p$
$\Diamond \, \triangle \, \mathrm{P} \, 6_p$
$\mathbb{C} \, \bullet \, \mathrm{Q} \, 11_p$

$\mathbb{C} \, \bullet \, \hat{\delta} \, 10^a$

$\sigma^{\!} \, \sigma \, \mathrm{2\!\!\!I} \, 7^a$ $\mathbb{C} \, \sigma \, \Diamond \, 7^a$

Planet positions in zodiac

☿	Mercury	♉	(R)
♀	Venus	♓ 28	♈
♂	Mars	♓	
♃	Jupiter	♓	
♄	Saturn	♑	
⛢	Uranus	♈	
♆	Neptune	♓	
♇	Pluto	♐	(R)

Planet (naked eye) visibility

Evening:
—

All night:
—

Morning:
Venus, Mars, Jupiter, Saturn

Pisces	♈ Aries	♉ Taurus	♊ Gemini	♋ Cancer	♌ Leo		
Virgo	♎ Libra	♏ Scorpio	♐ Sagittarius	♑ Capricorn	♒ Aquarius		

Control pests
(see p. 74 for details)

- **Flies:** burn fly papers in the cow barn at Flower times.
- **Moths:** ash from May 24 3^a to May 27 1^a.
- **Mole crickets:** ash from May 16 4^a to May 18 5^a.
- **Chitinous insects, wheat weevil, Colorado beetle and varroa:** ash from May 29 1^a to May 31 11_p.

Southern hemisphere

Southern Transplanting Time
May 18 11_p to June 1

My notes

Tip

Not sure what type of plant your vegetable is?
- See Crop tables, p. 66

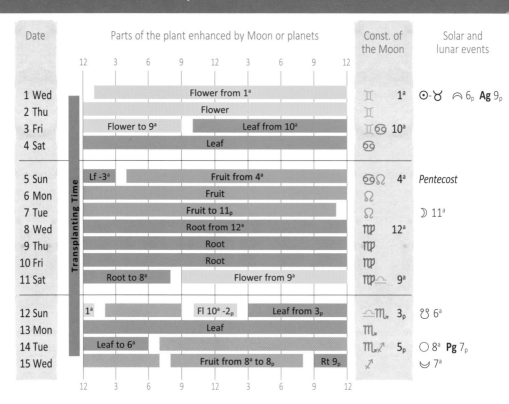

Date	Parts of the plant enhanced by Moon or planets	Const. of the Moon	Solar and lunar events
	12 3 6 9 12 3 6 9 12		
1 Wed	Flower from 1ᵃ	♊ 1ᵃ	☉-♉ ⌢ 6ₚ **Ag** 9ₚ
2 Thu	Flower	♊	
3 Fri	Flower to 9ᵃ Leaf from 10ᵃ	♊♋ 10ᵃ	
4 Sat	Leaf	♋	
5 Sun	Lf -3ᵃ Fruit from 4ᵃ	♋♌ 4ᵃ	Pentecost
6 Mon	Fruit	♌	
7 Tue	Fruit to 11ₚ	♌	☽ 11ᵃ
8 Wed	Root from 12ᵃ	♍ 12ᵃ	
9 Thu	Root	♍	
10 Fri	Root	♍	
11 Sat	Root to 8ᵃ Flower from 9ᵃ	♍⌢ 9ᵃ	
12 Sun	1ᵃ Fl 10ᵃ -2ₚ Leaf from 3ₚ	⌢♏ 3ₚ	☍ 6ᵃ
13 Mon	Leaf	♏	
14 Tue	Leaf to 6ᵃ	♏♐ 5ₚ	◯ 8ᵃ **Pg** 7ₚ
15 Wed	Fruit from 8ᵃ to 8ₚ Rt 9ₚ	♐	⌣ 7ᵃ
	12 3 6 9 12 3 6 9 12		

(Transplanting Time — vertical label spanning June 1–11)

Transplanting Time
(time of descending Moon in northern hemisphere)
June 1 8ₚ to June 15 5ᵃ and June 29 2ᵃ to July 12

Fruit times

- Tend fruit plants (beans, grains, tomatoes) during these times.
- Sow beans, cucumbers, zucchini (courgettes).

Leaf times
- Tend leafy plants (like lettuce) during these times.
- Thin and/or transplant any lettuce, Brussels sprouts, cabbage, kale, etc. that need it.
- Cut aromatic herbs before they bloom.

Flower times
- Tend flowering plants (broccoli, roses) during these times.
- Cut **hay.**
- Pick flowers for teas and dry them in the dark.
- Layer wisteria and trumpet vines.
- Thin or transplant cauliflowers, broccoli.

Root times

- Tend root plants (carrots, potatoes) during these times.
- Sow winter radishes, rutabaga (swedes), parsnips and carrots for fall harvesting.

Beekeeping

Begin **queen bee** rearing (grafting or larval transfer, comb insertion, cell punching) at Flower times.

ate	My notes

Planetary aspects
(**Bold** = visible to naked eye)

1

2

3 ☽ ☌ ♇ 11ᵃ

4

5 ☽ ☌ ♄ 5ₚ

6

7

8 ☽ ☌ ♆ 3ᵃ ☽ ☌ ♃ 8ₚ

9 ☽ ☌ ♂ 8ᵃ

0 ☿ △ ♇ 5ₚ

1 ♀ ☌ ⛢ 7ₚ ☽ ☌ ⛢ 9ₚ ☽ ☌ ♀ 9ₚ

2 ☽ ☌ ☿ 6ₚ

3

4

5

Planet positions in zodiac

☿ Mercury ♉ (R 3 D)

♀ Venus ♈

♂ Mars ♓

♃ Jupiter ♓

♄ Saturn ♑ (4 R)

⛢ Uranus ♈

♆ Neptune ♓

♇ Pluto ♐ (R)

Planet (naked eye) visibility

Evening:
–

All night:
Saturn

Morning:
Venus, Mars, Jupiter

♓ Pisces	♈ Aries	♉ Taurus	♊ Gemini	♋ Cancer	♌ Leo
♍ Virgo	♎ Libra	♏ Scorpio	♐ Sagittarius	♑ Capricorn	♒ Aquarius

B: All zodiac symbols refer to astronomical constellations, not astrological signs (see p. 10)

Control pests
(see p. 74 for details)

- **Flies:** burn fly papers at Flower times.
- **Mole crickets:** ash from June 12 3ₚ to June 14 4ₚ.
- **Ants** in the house: ash when the Moon is in Leo, June 5 4ᵃ to June 7 11ₚ.

Southern hemisphere

Southern Transplanting Time
May 18 to June 1 4ₚ and June 15 9ᵃ to June 28 10ₚ

My notes

My notes

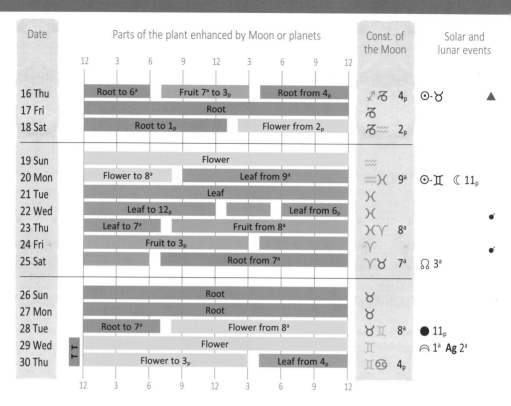

Date	Parts of the plant enhanced by Moon or planets	Const. of the Moon	Solar and lunar events
16 Thu	Root to 6a / Fruit 7a to 3p / Root from 4p	♐ ♑ 4p	☉-♉ ▲
17 Fri	Root	♑	
18 Sat	Root to 1p / Flower from 2p	♑ ♒ 2p	
19 Sun	Flower	♒	
20 Mon	Flower to 8a / Leaf from 9a	♒ ♓ 9a	☉-♊ ☾ 11p
21 Tue	Leaf	♓	
22 Wed	Leaf to 12p / Leaf from 6p	♓	
23 Thu	Leaf to 7a / Fruit from 8a	♓ ♈ 8a	
24 Fri	Fruit to 3p	♈	
25 Sat	Root from 7a	♈ ♉ 7a	☊ 3a
26 Sun	Root	♉	
27 Mon	Root	♉	
28 Tue	Root to 7a / Flower from 8a	♉ ♊ 8a	● 11p
29 Wed	Flower	♊	☋ 1a Ag 2a
30 Thu	Flower to 3p / Leaf from 4p	♊ ♋ 4p	

Time axis: 12 3 6 9 12 3 6 9 12

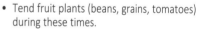

 (T T — 29 Wed)

Transplanting Time
(time of descending Moon in northern hemisphere)
June 29 2a to July 12

Leaf times

- Tend leafy plants (like lettuce) during these times.
- Cut aromatic herbs before they bloom.
- Mow lawns if you want to encourage vigorous growth of the grass.

Root times
- Tend root plants (carrots, potatoes) during these times.
- Harvest early potatoes as needed.
- Harvest onions, garlic, shallots, and dry before storing.

Fruit times
- Tend fruit plants (beans, grains, tomatoes) during these times.
- Harvest tomatoes.
- Sow zucchini (courgettes).
- Lightly prune fruit trees and shrubs.

Flower times
- Tend flowering plants (broccoli, roses) during these times.
- Cut **hay.**

Beekeeping
Begin **queen bee** rearing (grafting or larval transfer, comb insertion, cell punching) at Flower times.

te   My notes

Planetary aspects
(**Bold** = visible to naked eye)

⊙△♄ 3ᵃ ☾♂♇ 3ₚ

☾♂♄ 11ᵃ

☾♂♆ 3ₚ

♀△♇ 4ᵃ ☾♂♃ 12ₚ

☾●♂ 3ₚ

☾●♆ 6ₚ

☾♂♀ 3ᵃ

☾♂☿ 3ᵃ

☽♂♇ 4ₚ

Planet positions in zodiac

☿	Mercury	♉
♀	Venus	♈ 17 ♉
♂	Mars	♓
♃	Jupiter	♓
♄	Saturn	♑ (R)
♅	Uranus	♈
♆	Neptune	♓ (28 R)
♇	Pluto	♐ (R)

Planet (naked eye) visibility

Evening:
–

All night:
Saturn

Morning:
Venus, Mars, Jupiter

Pisces	♈ Aries	♉ Taurus	♊ Gemini	♋ Cancer	♌ Leo
Virgo	♎ Libra	♏ Scorpio	♐ Sagittarius	♑ Capricorn	♒ Aquarius

: All zodiac symbols refer to astronomical constellations, not astrological signs (see p. 10)

Control pests
(see p. 74 for details)

- **Chitinous insects, wheat weevil, Colorado beetle and varroa:** ash from June 25 7ᵃ to June 28 7ᵃ.
- **Flies:** burn fly papers at Flower times.
- **Grasshoppers:** ash from June 18 2ₚ to June 20 8ᵃ, and June 28 8ᵃ to June 30 3ₚ.

Biodynamic preparations

Look for the places where **valerian** is growing to save time searching for it when it comes to harvesting in July and August.

Tip

Want to know more about biodynamic preparations?
- See Biodynamic preparations, p. 73

Southern hemisphere

Southern Transplanting Time
June 15 to June 28 10ₚ

My notes

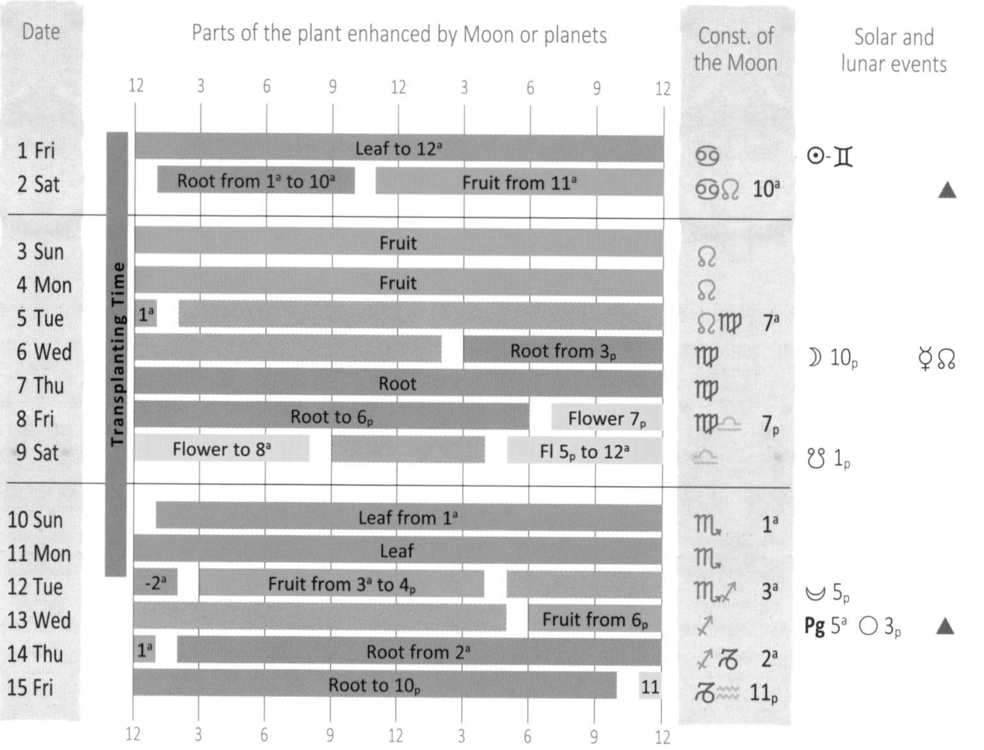
Date
Parts of the plant enhanced by Moon or planets
Const. of the Moon
Solar and lunar events
12 3 6 9 12 3 6 9 12
Transplanting Time
1 Fri
Leaf to 12^a
♋
☉-♊
2 Sat
Root from 1^a to 10^a
Fruit from 11^a
♋♌ 10^a
▲
3 Sun
Fruit
♌
4 Mon
Fruit
♌
5 Tue
1^a
♌♍ 7^a
6 Wed
Root from 3_p
♍
☽ 10_p
☿♌
7 Thu
Root
♍
8 Fri
Root to 6_p
Flower 7_p
♍♎ 7_p
9 Sat
Flower to 8^a
Fl 5_p to 12^a
♎
☋ 1_p
10 Sun
Leaf from 1^a
♏ 1^a
11 Mon
Leaf
♏
12 Tue
-2^a
Fruit from 3^a to 4_p
♏♐ 3^a
◡ 5_p
13 Wed
Fruit from 6_p
♐
Pg 5^a ○ 3_p
▲
14 Thu
1^a
Root from 2^a
♐♑ 2^a
15 Fri
Root to 10_p
11
♑♒ 11_p
12 3 6 9 12 3 6 9 12

Transplanting Time
(time of descending Moon in northern hemisphere)
June 29 to July 12 3_p and July 26 7^a to Aug 9

Leaf times

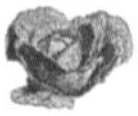

- Tend leafy plants (like lettuce) during these times.
- Harvest **seeds of leaf plants** to be used for seed from June 30 4_p to July 1 11_p and at other Leaf times, avoiding unfavorable times.
- Spray leaf plants and the soil with horn silica early in the morning.

Root times

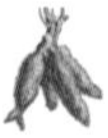

- Tend root plants (carrots, potatoes) during these times.
- Harvest **seeds of root plants** to be used for seed from July 6 3_p to July 8 6_p and at other Root times, avoiding unfavorable times.

Fruit times

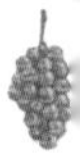

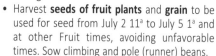

- Tend fruit plants (beans, grains, tomatoes) during these times.
- Harvest **seeds of fruit plants** and **grain** to be used for seed from July 2 11^a to July 5 1^a and at other Fruit times, avoiding unfavorable times. Sow climbing and pole (runner) beans.
- Prune tomato suckers or side shoots.

Flower times

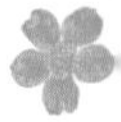

- Tend flowering plants (broccoli, roses) during these times.
- Harvest **seeds of flower plants** to be used for seed from July 8 7_p to July 9 11_p and at other Flower times, avoiding unfavorable times.
- Cut **late hay.**
- Sow biennials such as pansies, and perenniels like hyssop, columbine, etc.

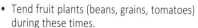

Date   My notes

Planetary aspects
(**Bold** = visible to naked eye)

	Planet positions in zodiac
☿	Mercury ♉ 4 ♊
♀	Venus ♉
♂	Mars ♓ 4 ♈
♃	Jupiter ♓
♄	Saturn ♑ (R)
♅	Uranus ♈
♆	Neptune ♓ (R)
♇	Pluto ♐ (R)

1
2   ☿△♄ 7ᵃ ☽☌♄ 10ₚ
3
4
5   ☽☌♆ 10ᵃ
6   ☿♌ 2ᵃ ☽☌♃ 9ᵃ
7
8   ☽☌♂ 5ᵃ
9   ☽☌♅ 9ᵃ
10
11   ☽☌♀ 5ₚ
12
13   ♀△♄ 1ᵃ ☽☌☿ 8ᵃ
14   ☾☌♇ 1ᵃ
15   ☾☌♄ 6ₚ

Planet (naked eye) visibility

Evening:
–

All night:
Saturn

Morning:
Venus, Mars, Jupiter

♓ Pisces	♈ Aries	♉ Taurus	♊ Gemini	♋ Cancer	♌ Leo
♍ Virgo	♎ Libra	♏ Scorpio	♐ Sagittarius	♑ Capricorn	♒ Aquarius

NB: All zodiac symbols refer to astronomical constellations, not astrological signs (see p. 10)

Control pests
(see p. 74 for details)

- **Flies:** burn fly papers at Flower times.
- **Slugs:** ash from June 30 4ₚ to July 1 11ₚ. Spray leaf plants and the soil with horn silica early in the morning during Leaf times.
- **Ants** in the house: ash when the Moon is in Leo, July 2 10ᵃ to July 5 6ᵃ.

Southern hemisphere

Southern Transplanting Time
July 12 7ₚ to July 26 3ᵃ

My notes

Biodynamic preparations

Pick **valerian** flowers at Flower times early in the morning while there is still plenty of night-time moisture around. The juice should be pressed out immediately without adding any water or leaving the plants in water. Juice to which water has been added will not keep long.

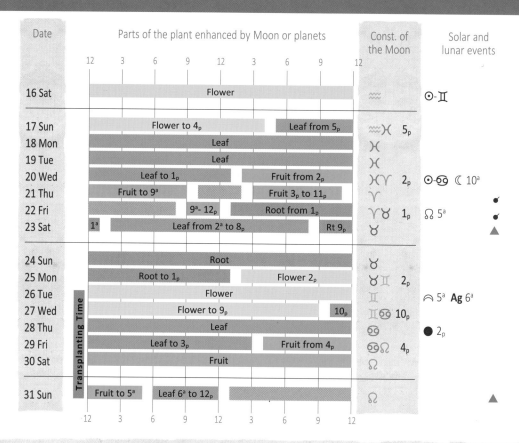

Date	Parts of the plant enhanced by Moon or planets (12 · 3 · 6 · 9 · 12 · 3 · 6 · 9 · 12)	Const. of the Moon	Solar and lunar events
16 Sat	Flower	≈	☉-♊
17 Sun	Flower to 4ₚ / Leaf from 5ₚ	≈ ⬦ ♓ 5ₚ	
18 Mon	Leaf	♓	
19 Tue	Leaf	♓	
20 Wed	Leaf to 1ₚ / Fruit from 2ₚ	♓♈ 2ₚ	☉-♋ ☾ 10ᵃ
21 Thu	Fruit to 9ᵃ / Fruit 3ₚ to 11ₚ	♈	
22 Fri	9ᵃ- 12ₚ / Root from 1ₚ	♈♉ 1ₚ	☊ 5ᵃ
23 Sat	1ᵃ / Leaf from 2ᵃ to 8ₚ / Rt 9ₚ	♉	▲
24 Sun	Root	♉	
25 Mon	Root to 1ₚ / Flower 2ₚ	♉♊ 2ₚ	
26 Tue	Flower	♊	⌢ 5ᵃ **Ag** 6ᵃ
27 Wed	Flower to 9ₚ / 10ₚ	♊♋ 10ₚ	
28 Thu	Leaf	♋	● 2ₚ
29 Fri	Leaf to 3ₚ / Fruit from 4ₚ	♋♌ 4ₚ	
30 Sat	Fruit	♌	
31 Sun	Fruit to 5ᵃ / Leaf 6ᵃ to 12ₚ	♌	▲

(Transplanting Time shown as a vertical bar spanning July 26–31)

Transplanting Time
(time of descending Moon in northern hemisphere)
July 26 7ᵃ to Aug 9

Leaf times

- Tend leafy plants (like lettuce) during these times.
- Harvest **seeds of leaf plants** to be used for seed from July 17 5ₚ to July 20 1ₚ.
- Spray leaf plants and the soil with horn silica early in the morning.

Root times

- Tend root plants (carrots, potatoes) during these times.
- Harvest **seeds of root plants** to be used for seed from July 22 1ₚ to July 23 1ᵃ and July 23 9ₚ to July 25 1ₚ.

Fruit times

- Tend fruit plants (beans, grains, tomatoes) during these times.
- Harvest **seeds of fruit plants** and **grain** to be used for seed from July 29 4ₚ to July 31 5ᵃ and at other Fruit times, avoiding unfavorable times.
- Cut raspberry canes that have finished bearing fruit.

Flower times

- Tend flowering plants (broccoli, roses) during these times.
- Harvest **seeds of flower plants** to be used for seed from July 25 2ₚ to July 27 9ₚ and at other Flower times, avoiding unfavorable times.
- Cut **late hay.**
- Plant fall flowering bulbs.
- Graft rosehips.

ate	My notes	Planetary aspects (**Bold** = visible to naked eye)
6		$\odot\sigma\,\xi\;4_p$
7		$\xi\triangle\Psi\;4^a\quad\odot\triangle\Psi\;7_p\quad\mathbb{C}\sigma\Psi\;11_p$
8		$\xi\sigma^o\mathrm{P}\;3^a\quad\mathbb{C}\sigma\,2\!\!\!\!4\;11_p$
9		$\odot\sigma^o\mathrm{P}\;9_p$
0		
1		$\mathbb{C}\bullet\sigma^{\!\!\!'}\;12_p$
2		$\mathbb{C}\bullet\hat{\delta}\;2^a$
3		$\xi\triangle\,2\!\!\!\!4\;2_p$
4		
5		
6		$\mathbb{C}\sigma\,\varphi\;11^a$
7		$\mathbb{C}\sigma^o\mathrm{P}\;9_p$
8		
9		$\mathbb{D}\sigma\,\xi\;8_p$
0		$\mathbb{D}\sigma^o\hbar\;1^a$
1		$\xi\sigma^o\hbar\;2^a\quad\odot\triangle\,2\!\!\!\!4\;6_p$

Planet positions in zodiac

☿ Mercury	♊ 18 ♋
	28 ♌
♀ Venus	♉ 17 ♊
♂ Mars	♈
♃ Jupiter	♓ (28 R)
♄ Saturn	♑ (R)
♅ Uranus	♈
♆ Neptune	♓ (R)
♇ Pluto	♐ (R)

Planet (naked eye) visibility

Evening:
–

All night:
Saturn

Morning:
Venus, Mars, Jupiter

B: All zodiac symbols refer to astronomical constellations, not astrological signs (see p. 10)

Control pests
(see p. 74 for details)

- **Flies:** burn fly papers at Flower times.
- **Slugs:** ash from July 27 10_p to July 29 3_p. Spray leaf plants and the soil with horn silica early in the morning during Leaf times.
- **Grasshoppers:** ash July 25 2_p to July 27 9_p. **Ants** in the house: ash when the Moon is in Leo, July 29 4_p to Aug 1 11^a.

Biodynamic preparations

Pick **Valerian** flowers at Flower times early in the morning while there is still plenty of night-time moisture around. The juice should be pressed out immediately without adding any water or leaving the plants in water. Juice to which water has been added will not keep long.

Southern hemisphere

Southern Transplanting Time
July 12 to July 26 3^a

Maria Thun's tree log preparations

- Cut **larch** logs, fill with dried **camomile** and put them into the ground between July 17 4_p and July 18 9^a or between July 30 3_p and July 31 8^a.
- Cut **maple** logs, fill with dried **dandelion** and put them into the ground between July 19 10^a and July 20 3^a.

Tip

Want to know more about biodynamic preparations?
- See Biodynamic preparations, p. 73

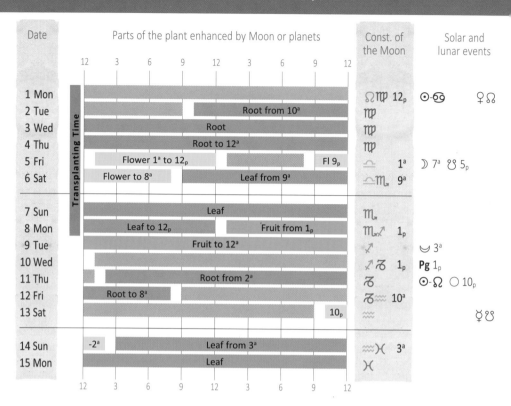

Date	Parts of the plant enhanced by Moon or planets	Const. of the Moon	Solar and lunar events
1 Mon	Transplanting Time	♌♍ 12ₚ	☉·♋ ♀♌
2 Tue	Root from 10ᵃ	♍	
3 Wed	Root	♍	
4 Thu	Root to 12ᵃ	♍	
5 Fri	Flower 1ᵃ to 12ₚ Fl 9ₚ	♎ 1ᵃ	☽ 7ᵃ ♋ 5ₚ
6 Sat	Flower to 8ᵃ Leaf from 9ᵃ	♎♏ 9ᵃ	
7 Sun	Leaf	♏	
8 Mon	Leaf to 12ₚ Fruit from 1ₚ	♏♐ 1ₚ	
9 Tue	Fruit to 12ᵃ	♐	☽ 3ᵃ
10 Wed		♐♑ 1ₚ	**Pg** 1ₚ
11 Thu	Root from 2ᵃ	♑	☉·♌ ○ 10ₚ
12 Fri	Root to 8ᵃ	♑♒ 10ᵃ	
13 Sat	10ₚ	♒	☿♌
14 Sun	-2ᵃ Leaf from 3ᵃ	♒♓ 3ᵃ	
15 Mon	Leaf	♓	

Transplanting Time
(time of descending Moon in northern hemisphere)
July 26 to Aug 9 1ᵃ and Aug 22 1ₚ to Sep 5

Leaf times

- Tend leafy plants (like lettuce) during these times.
- Harvest **seeds of leaf plants** to be used for seed from Aug 6 9ᵃ to Aug 8 12ₚ and from Aug 14 3ᵃ to Aug 16 1ᵃ.
- Sow weather hardy lamb's lettuce and cabbage.

Root times
- Tend root plants (carrots, potatoes).
- Harvest **seeds of root plants** to be used for seed from Aug 2 10ᵃ to Aug 4 11ₚ and from Aug 11 2ᵃ to Aug 12 8ᵃ.
- Harvest carrots, onions, potatoes.

Fruit times
- Tend fruit plants (beans, grains, tomatoes) during these times.
- Harvest **seeds of fruit plants** and **grain** to be used for seed from Aug 8 1ₚ to Aug 9 11ₚ and at other Fruit times, avoiding unfavorable times.
- Immediately after harvest, sow catch crops like lupins, phacelia, mustard or wild flax.
- After the harvest prune fruit trees.

Flower times

- Tend flowering plants (broccoli, roses) during these times.
- Harvest **seeds of flower plants** to be used for seed, but best in second half of the month, when there is a longer uninterrupted Flower time.
- Prune roses.

| te | My notes |

Planetary aspects
(**Bold** = visible to naked eye)

$\mathcal{D} \, \varpi \, \Psi \, 3_p \quad \sigma \, \sigma \, \hat{\delta} \, 8_p \quad \varphi \, \mathcal{\Omega} \, 9_p$

$\mathcal{D} \, \varpi \, 4 \, 4_p$

$\mathcal{D} \, \varpi \, \hat{\delta} \, 5_p \quad \mathcal{D} \, \varpi \, \sigma \, 10_p$

$\varphi \, \triangle \, \Psi \, 1_p$

$\varphi \, \varpi \, \mathbf{P} \, 1^a$

$\mathcal{D} \, \sigma \, \mathbf{P} \, 10^a \quad \mathcal{D} \, \varpi \, \varphi \, 1_p$

$\mathbb{C} \, \sigma \, \hbar \, 2^a$

$\varnothing \, \mathcal{U} \, 9^a \quad \mathbb{C} \, \varpi \, \varnothing \, 3_p$

$\mathbb{C} \, \sigma \, \Psi \, 8^a \quad \odot \, \varpi \, \hbar \, 1_p \quad \sigma \, \triangle \, \mathbf{P} \, 3_p$

$\mathbb{C} \, \sigma \, 4 \, 7^a$

Planet positions in zodiac

☿	Mercury	♌	
♀	Venus	♊	9 ♋
♂	Mars	♈	9 ♉
♃	Jupiter	♓	(R)
♄	Saturn	♑	(R)
♅	Uranus	♈	
♆	Neptune	♓	(R)
♇	Pluto	♐	(R)

Planet (naked eye) visibility

Evening:
–

All night:
Jupiter, Saturn

Morning:
Venus, Mars

| Pisces | ♈ Aries | ♉ Taurus | ♊ Gemini | ♋ Cancer | ♌ Leo |
| Virgo | ♎ Libra | ♏ Scorpio | ♐ Sagittarius | ♑ Capricorn | ♒ Aquarius |

: All zodiac symbols refer to astronomical constellations, not astrological signs (see p. 10)

Control pests
(see p. 74 for details)

- **Flies:** burn fly papers at Flower times.
- **Ants** in the house: ash when the Moon is in Leo, July 29 4_p to Aug 1 11^a.

Maria Thun's tree log preparations

- Cut **birch** logs, fill with dried **yarrow** and put them into the ground between Aug 8 2_p and Aug 9 7^a.
- Cut **maple** logs, fill with dried **dandelion** and put them into the ground between Aug 14 2^a and 7_p.

Tip

Not sure what type of plant your vegetable is?
- See Crop tables, p. 66

Southern hemisphere

Southern Transplanting Time
Aug 9 5^a to Aug 22 9^a

My notes

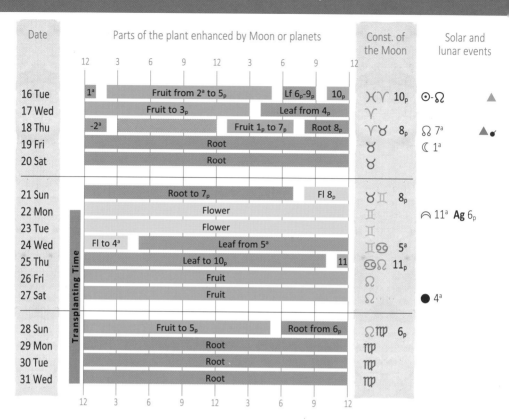

Date	Parts of the plant enhanced by Moon or planets	Const. of the Moon	Solar and lunar events
	12 3 6 9 12 3 6 9 12		
16 Tue	1ᵃ Fruit from 2ᵃ to 5ₚ Lf 6ₚ-9ₚ 10ₚ	♓♈ 10ₚ	☉-♌ ▲
17 Wed	Fruit to 3ₚ Leaf from 4ₚ	♈	
18 Thu	-2ᵃ Fruit 1ₚ to 7ₚ Root 8ₚ	♈♉ 8ₚ	♌ 7ᵃ ▲◗
19 Fri	Root	♉	☾ 1ᵃ
20 Sat	Root	♉	
21 Sun	Root to 7ₚ Fl 8ₚ	♉♊ 8ₚ	
22 Mon	Flower	♊	⌂ 11ᵃ **Ag** 6ₚ
23 Tue	Flower	♊	
24 Wed	Fl to 4ᵃ Leaf from 5ᵃ	♊♋ 5ᵃ	
25 Thu	Leaf to 10ₚ 11	♋♌ 11ₚ	
26 Fri	Fruit	♌	
27 Sat	Fruit	♌	● 4ᵃ
28 Sun	Fruit to 5ₚ Root from 6ₚ	♌♍ 6ₚ	
29 Mon	Root	♍	
30 Tue	Root	♍	
31 Wed	Root	♍	
	12 3 6 9 12 3 6 9 12		

Transplanting Time (vertical, spanning Aug 21–31)

Transplanting Time
(time of descending Moon in northern hemisphere)
Aug 22 1ₚ to Sep 5

Leaf times

- Tend leafy plants (like lettuce) during these times.
- Harvest **seeds of leaf plants** to be used for seed from Aug 14 3ᵃ to Aug 16 1ᵃ and from Aug 24 5ᵃ to Aug 25 10ₚ.
- Mow lawns if you want to encourage vigorous growth of the grass.

Root times

- Tend root plants (carrots, potatoes) during these times.
- Harvest **seeds of leaf plants** to be used for seed from Aug 18 8ₚ to Aug 21 7ₚ and from Aug 28 6ₚ to Sep 1 6ᵃ.

Fruit times

- Tend fruit plants (beans, grains, tomatoes) during these times.
- Harvest **seeds of fruit plants** and **grain** to be used for seed from Aug 25 11ₚ to Aug 28 5ₚ and at other Fruit times, avoiding unfavorable times.
- Immediately after harvest, sow catch crops like lupins, phacelia, mustard or wild flax.

Flower times

- Tend flowering plants (broccoli, roses) during these times.
- Harvest **seeds of flower plants** to be used for seed from Aug 21 8ₚ to Aug 24 4ᵃ.
- Sow hardy annuals for early bloom next spring.
- Graft rosehips.

ate	My notes	Planetary aspects (**Bold** = visible to naked eye)
6		☿△♅ 2_p
7		
8		♀△♃ 4^a ☾☌♅ 10^a
9		**☾☌♂ 7^a**
0		
1		☿☍♆ 4^a
2		☿△♇ 6_p
3		
4		☾☍♇ 2^a
5		**☾☌♀ 8_p**
6		☾☍♄ 3^a
7		
8		♀☍♄ 2_p ☽☍♆ 7_p
9		☽☌☿ 12_p ☽☍♃ 7_p
0		
1		

Planet positions in zodiac

☿ Mercury	♌	20 ♍
♀ Venus	♋	26 ♌
♂ Mars	♉	
♃ Jupiter	♓	(R)
♄ Saturn	♑	(R)
♅ Uranus	♈	(24 R)
♆ Neptune	♓	(R)
♇ Pluto	♐	(R)

Planet (naked eye) visibility

Evening:
–

All night:
Jupiter, Saturn

Morning:
Venus, Mars

♓ Pisces ♈ Aries ♉ Taurus ♊ Gemini ♋ Cancer ♌ Leo
♍ Virgo ♎ Libra ♏ Scorpio ♐ Sagittarius ♑ Capricorn ♒ Aquarius

Control pests
(see p. 74 for details)

- **Flies:** burn fly papers at Flower times.
- **Ants** in the house: ash when the Moon is in Leo, Aug 25 11_p to Aug 28 5_p.

Biodynamic preparations

Cut **yarrow** in the mornings at Fruit times. The blossoms should show some seed formation.

Maria Thun's tree log preparations

- Cut **larch** logs, fill with dried **camomile** and put them into the ground between Aug 20 5_p and Aug 21 10^a.
- Cut **birch** logs, fill with dried **yarrow** and put them into the ground on Aug 28 between 3^a and 8_p.

Southern hemisphere

Southern Transplanting Time
Aug 9 to Aug 22 9^a

My notes

Date	Parts of the plant enhanced by Moon or planets	Const. of the Moon	Solar and lunar events
	12 3 6 9 12 3 6 9 12		
1 Thu	Root to 6ᵃ Fl 7ᵃ – 12ₚ Fl 9ₚ	♍︎♎︎ 7ᵃ	☉-♌︎ ☋ 5ₚ
2 Fri	Flower to 2ₚ Leaf from 3ₚ	♎︎♏︎ 3ₚ	
3 Sat	Leaf	♏︎	☽ 2ₚ
4 Sun	Leaf to 7ₚ Fruit 8ₚ	♏︎♐︎ 8ₚ	
5 Mon	Fruit	♐︎	☽ 10ᵃ
6 Tue	Fruit to 9ₚ 10ₚ	♐︎♑︎ 10ₚ	
7 Wed	1ᵃ	♑︎	**Pg** 2ₚ
8 Thu	Root from 3ᵃ to 7ₚ Flower 8ₚ	♑︎♒︎ 8ₚ	
9 Fri	Flower from 0ᵃ	♒︎	
10 Sat	Flower to 12ₚ Leaf from 1ₚ	♒︎♓︎ 1ₚ	○ 6ᵃ
11 Sun	-2ᵃ Fruit 3ᵃ to 12ₚ Leaf from 1ₚ	♓︎	▲
12 Mon	Leaf	♓︎	
13 Tue	Leaf to 6ᵃ Fruit from 7ᵃ	♓︎♈︎ 7ᵃ	
14 Wed	Fruit to 6ᵃ 10ₚ	♈︎	♌︎ 11ᵃ
15 Thu	Fr -3ᵃ Root from 4ᵃ	♈︎♉︎ 4ᵃ	
	12 3 6 9 12 3 6 9 12		

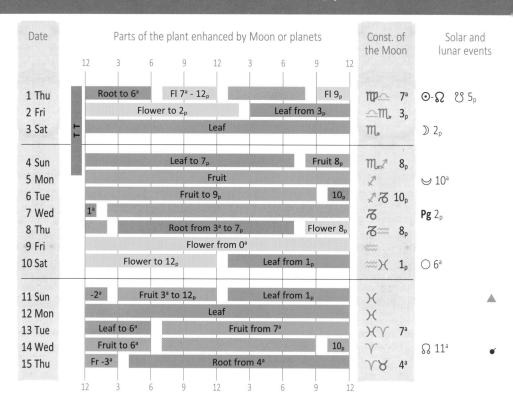

Transplanting Time
(time of descending Moon in northern hemisphere)
Aug 22 to Sep 5 8ᵃ and Sep 18 8ₚ to Oct 2

Leaf times

- Tend leafy plants (like lettuce) during these times.

Root times
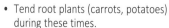
- Tend root plants (carrots, potatoes) during these times.
- The harvest of **root crops** is always best undertaken at Root times. Storage trials of onions, carrots, beets (beetroots) and potatoes have demonstrated this time and again.

Fruit times
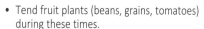
- Tend fruit plants (beans, grains, tomatoes) during these times.
- Good times to **harvest fruit** are when the Moon is in Sagittarius or Aries (Sep 4 8ₚ to Sep 6 9ₚ, and Sep 13 7ᵃ to Sep 15 3ᵃ), or other Fruit times, always avoiding unfavorable times.
- Good times for **sowing winter grain** are when the Moon is in Leo or Sagittarius (Sep 4 8ₚ to Sep 6 9ₚ, and Sep 22 to Sep 24) avoiding unfavorable times, and at other Fruit times.
- **Rye** can, if necessary, also be sown at Root times with all subsequent cultivations being carried out at Fruit times.

Flower times

- Tend flowering plants (broccoli, roses) during these times.
- During Transplanting Time transplant annuals and bienniels that were sown earlier.

te   My notes

Planetary aspects
(**Bold** = visible to naked eye)

$D\,\sigma^o\,\hat{\delta}\,11_p$

$\ddot{\varphi}\,\sigma^o\,2\!\!\!\!4\,10_p$

$D\,\sigma^o\,\sigma'\,8^a$

$D\,\sigma\,P\,6_p$

$D\,\sigma\,\hbar\,9^a$

$D\,\sigma^o\,\varphi\,10^a$

$\mathbb{C}\,\sigma\,\Psi\,5_p$

$\odot\,\triangle\,\hat{\delta}\,9^a$ $\mathbb{C}\,\sigma\,2\!\!\!\!4\,1_p$ $\mathbb{C}\,\sigma^o\,\ddot{\varphi}\,6_p$

$\mathbb{C}\,\bullet\,\hat{\delta}\,7_p$

Planet positions in zodiac

☿	Mercury	♍ (10 R)
♀	Venus	♌
♂	Mars	♉
♃	Jupiter	♓ (R)
♄	Saturn	♑ (R)
♅	Uranus	♈ (R)
♆	Neptune	♓ (R)
♇	Pluto	♐ (R)

Planet (naked eye) visibility

Evening:
  –

All night:
  Mars, Jupiter, Saturn

Morning:
  Venus

Pisces	♈ Aries	♉ Taurus	♊ Gemini	♋ Cancer	♌ Leo
Virgo	♎ Libra	♏ Scorpio	♐ Sagittarius	♑ Capricorn	♒ Aquarius

: All zodiac symbols refer to astronomical constellations, not astrological signs (see p. 10)

Control pests
(see p. 74 for details)
• **Flies:** burn fly papers at Flower times.

Southern hemisphere
Southern Transplanting Time
Sep 5 12$_p$ to Sep 18 4$_p$

Biodynamic preparations
Cut **yarrow** in the mornings at Fruit times before Sep 15. The blossoms should show some seed formation.

My notes

My notes

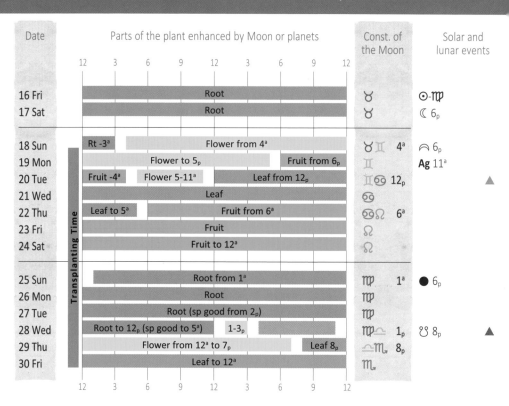

Date	Parts of the plant enhanced by Moon or planets	Const. of the Moon	Solar and lunar events
16 Fri	Root	♉	☉-♍
17 Sat	Root	♉	☾ 6ₚ
18 Sun	Rt -3ᵃ / Flower from 4ᵃ	♉♊ 4ᵃ	⌃ 6ₚ
19 Mon	Flower to 5ₚ / Fruit from 6ₚ	♊	Ag 11ᵃ
20 Tue	Fruit -4ᵃ / Flower 5-11ᵃ / Leaf from 12ₚ	♊♋ 12ₚ	▲
21 Wed	Leaf	♋	
22 Thu	Leaf to 5ᵃ / Fruit from 6ᵃ	♋♌ 6ᵃ	
23 Fri	Fruit	♌	
24 Sat	Fruit to 12ᵃ	♌	
25 Sun	Root from 1ᵃ	♍ 1ᵃ	● 6ₚ
26 Mon	Root	♍	
27 Tue	Root (sp good from 2ₚ)	♍	
28 Wed	Root to 12ₚ (sp good to 5ᵃ) / 1-3ₚ	♍♎ 1ₚ	☊ 8ₚ / ▲
29 Thu	Flower from 12ᵃ to 7ₚ / Leaf 8ₚ	♎♏ 8ₚ	
30 Fri	Leaf to 12ᵃ	♏	

(left margin, rows 18–30: **Transplanting Time**)

Transplanting Time
(time of descending Moon in northern hemisphere)
Sep 18 8ₚ to Oct 2

Leaf times

- Tend leafy plants (like lettuce) during these times.
- Plant conifer and evergreen shrubs.

Root times

- Tend root plants (carrots, potatoes) during these times.
- The harvest of **root crops** is always best undertaken at Root times. Storage trials of onions, carrots, beets (beetroots) and potatoes have demonstrated this time and again.
- Sow radishes in a cold frame.

Fruit times
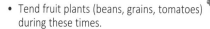
- Tend fruit plants (beans, grains, tomatoes) during these times.
- Good times to **harvest fruit** are when the Moon is in Sagittarius or Aries, or other Fruit times (Sep 22 6ᵃ to Sep 24 11ₚ) always avoiding unfavorable times.
- Good times for **sowing winter grain** are when the Moon is in Leo or Sagittarius (Sep 5 to 7, and Sep 22 6ᵃ to Sep 24 11ₚ).
- **Rye** can, if necessary, also be sown at Root times with all subsequent cultivations being carried out at Fruit times.

Flower times

- Tend flowering plants (broccoli, roses) during these times.
- During Transplanting Time transplant annuals and bienniels that were sown earlier.

te	My notes	Planetary aspects

(Bold = visible to naked eye)

Planet positions in zodiac

☿	Mercury	♍	(R)
♀	Venus	♌	24 ♍
♂	Mars	♉	
♃	Jupiter	♓	(R)
♄	Saturn	♑	(R)
⛢	Uranus	♈	(R)
♆	Neptune	♓	(R)
♇	Pluto	♐	(R)

Planetary aspects column (by date rows):

⊙☍♆ 6ₚ ☽☌♂ 9ₚ

☿☍♃ 7ₚ
⊙△♇ 1ᵃ
♀△⛢ 1ᵃ ☽☍♇ 9ᵃ

☽☍♄ 7ᵃ
⊙☌☿ 3ᵃ
♀☍♆ 5ᵃ

☽☍♆ 1ᵃ ☽☌♀ 3ᵃ ☽☌☿ 9ᵃ ☽☍♃ 8ₚ
♀△♇ 2ᵃ ☿☌♀ 2ₚ ⊙☍♃ 3ₚ
☿△♇ 9ᵃ
♂△♄ 2ᵃ
☽☍⛢ 4ᵃ

Planet (naked eye) visibility

Evening: –

All night:
Mars, Jupiter, Saturn

Morning:
Mercury (from Sep 30),
Venus

Pisces	♈ Aries	♉ Taurus	♊ Gemini	♋ Cancer	♌ Leo
Virgo	♎ Libra	♏ Scorpio	♐ Sagittarius	♑ Capricorn	♒ Aquarius

3: All zodiac symbols refer to astronomical constellations, not astrological signs (see p. 10)

Control pests
(see p. 74 for details)

- **Flies:** burn fly papers at Flower times.
- **Slugs:** ash between Sep 20 12ₚ and Sep 22 3ₚ.

Maria Thun's tree log preparations

- Cut **maple** logs, fill with dried **dandelion** and put them into the ground between Sep 16 7ᵃ and 11ₚ.
- Cut **larch** logs, fill with dried **camomile** and put them into the ground between Sep 18 8ᵃ and Sep 19 1ᵃ.
- Cut **birch** logs, fill with dried **yarrow** and put them into the ground between Sep 23 6ₚ and Sep 24 11ᵃ.

Southern hemisphere

Southern Transplanting Time
Sep 5 to Sep 18 4ₚ

My notes

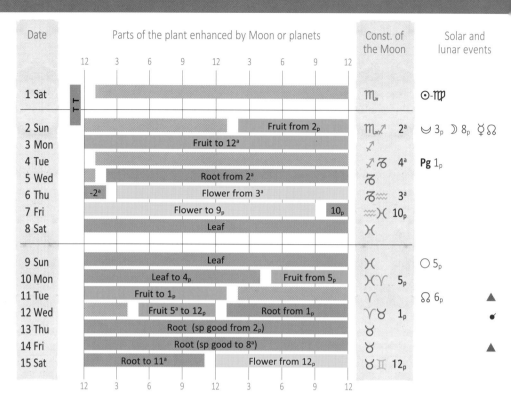

Date	Parts of the plant enhanced by Moon or planets	Const. of the Moon	Solar and lunar events
1 Sat	TT	♏	☉-♍
2 Sun	Fruit from 2p	♏♐ 2a	☾ 3p ☽ 8p ☿☊
3 Mon	Fruit to 12a	♐	
4 Tue		♐♑ 4a	**Pg** 1p
5 Wed	Root from 2a	♑	
6 Thu	-2a Flower from 3a	♑♒ 3a	
7 Fri	Flower to 9p 10p	♒♓ 10p	
8 Sat	Leaf	♓	
9 Sun	Leaf	♓	◯ 5p
10 Mon	Leaf to 4p Fruit from 5p	♓♈ 5p	
11 Tue	Fruit to 1p	♈	☊ 6p ▲
12 Wed	Fruit 5a to 12p Root from 1p	♈♉ 1p	☀
13 Thu	Root (sp good from 2p)	♉	
14 Fri	Root (sp good to 8a)	♉	▲
15 Sat	Root to 11a Flower from 12p	♉♊ 12p	

Transplanting Time
(time of descending Moon in northern hemisphere)
Sep 18 to Oct 2 1p and Oct 16 4a to Oct 29 7p

Fruit times
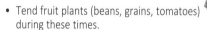
- Tend fruit plants (beans, grains, tomatoes) during these times.
- **Store fruit** at any Fruit or Flower time outside Transplanting Time.
- Harvest any ripe fruit.

Leaf times

- Tend leafy plants (like lettuce) during these times.
- Harvest **seeds of leaf plants.**
- Sow spinach, winter lettuce, lamb's lettuce (in a greenhouse if necessary).

Flower times

- Tend flowering plants (broccoli, roses) during these times.
- Harvest **seeds of flower plants.**
- Sow annual sweet peas in a greenhouse.

Root times
- Tend root plants (carrots, potatoes) during these times.
- Harvest **seeds of root plants.**
- In sunny regions sow radishes.

ate	My notes	Planetary aspects (**Bold** = visible to naked eye)

Planet positions in zodiac

☿	Mercury	♍	(R 2 D)
♀	Venus	♍	
♂	Mars	♉	
♃	Jupiter	♓	(R)
♄	Saturn	♑	(R)
♅	Uranus	♈	(R)
♆	Neptune	♓	(R)
♇	Pluto	♐	(R 8 D)

1 — ☽☌♂ 11ᵃ ♀☍♃ 2ₚ

2 — ☿☋ 1ᵃ

3 —

4 — ☽☌♇ 1ᵃ

5 — ☽☌♄ 2ₚ

6 —

7 — ☿△♇ 1ᵃ

8 — ☽☌♆ 1ᵃ ☽☍☿ 7ᵃ ☽☌♃ 4ₚ

9 — ☽☍♀ 10ᵃ

10 —

11 — ☉△♄ 9ₚ

12 — ☾●⚴ 2ᵃ ☿☍♃ 3ᵃ

13 —

14 — ♀△♄ 2ᵃ

15 — ☾☌♂ 1ᵃ

Planet (naked eye) visibility

Evening:
Saturn

All night:
Mars, Jupiter

Morning:
Mercury, Venus (to Oct 2)

♓	Pisces	♈	Aries	♉	Taurus	♊	Gemini	♋	Cancer	♌	Leo
♍	Virgo	♎	Libra	♏	Scorpio	♐	Sagittarius	♑	Capricorn	♒	Aquarius

NB: All zodiac symbols refer to astronomical constellations, not astrological signs (see p. 10)

Control pests
(see p. 74 for details)
- **Flies:** burn fly papers at Flower times.

Southern hemisphere
Southern Transplanting Time
Oct 2 5ₚ to Oct 15 11ₚ and Oct 29 11ₚ to Nov 12

Treating cleared ground
All **cleared ground** should be treated with compost and sprayed with barrel preparation, and plowed ready for winter.

My notes

My notes

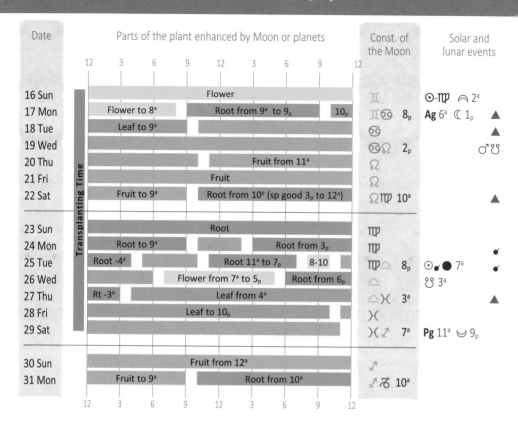

Date	Parts of the plant enhanced by Moon or planets	Const. of the Moon	Solar and lunar events
16 Sun	Flower	♊	☉-♍ ⌒ 2a
17 Mon	Flower to 8a / Root from 9a to 9p / 10p	♊♋ 8p	Ag 6a ☾ 1p ▲
18 Tue	Leaf to 9a	♋	▲
19 Wed		♋♌ 2p	♂☋
20 Thu	Fruit from 11a	♌	
21 Fri	Fruit	♌	
22 Sat	Fruit to 9a / Root from 10a (sp good 3p to 12a)	♌♍ 10a	▲
23 Sun	Root	♍	
24 Mon	Root to 9a / Root from 3p	♍	◞
25 Tue	Root -4a / Root 11a to 7p / 8-10	♍♎ 8p	☉ ● 7a ◞
26 Wed	Flower from 7a to 5p / Root from 6p	♎	☋ 3a
27 Thu	Rt -3a / Leaf from 4a	♎♓ 3a	▲
28 Fri	Leaf to 10p	♓	
29 Sat		♓♐ 7a	Pg 11a ☽ 9p
30 Sun	Fruit from 12a	♐	
31 Mon	Fruit to 9a / Root from 10a	♐♑ 10a	

Transplanting Time (vertical label, Oct 16–Oct 29)

Chart time scale: 12 3 6 9 12 3 6 9 12

Transplanting Time
(time of descending Moon in northern hemisphere)
Oct 16 4a to Oct 29 7p

Leaf times
- Tend leafy plants (like lettuce) during these times.
- Harvest **seeds of leaf plants.**
- Transplant conifer and evergreen shrubs.
- Transplant cabbage.

Root times
- Tend root plants (carrots, potatoes) during these times.
- Harvest **seeds of root plants.**
- Sow carrots, transplant onions.

Fruit times
- Tend fruit plants (beans, grains, tomatoes) during these times.
- **Store fruit** at any Fruit or Flower time outside Transplanting Time.
- Transplant strawberries.

Flower times

- Tend flowering plants (broccoli, roses) during these times.
- Harvest **seeds of flower plants.**
- Plant hyacinths, tulips and lilies.
- Transplant bienniels.

Treating cleared ground
All **cleared ground** should be treated with compost and sprayed with barrel preparation, and plowed ready for winter.

ate	My notes	Planetary aspects
		(**Bold** = visible to naked eye)

Planetary aspects

Date	Aspects
6	
7	☾ ☌ ♇ 5ₚ ☉ △ ♂ 6ₚ
8	♀ △ ♂ 10ₚ
9	☾ ☍ ♄ 2ₚ ♂ ☊ 10ₚ
0	
1	
2	☾ ☍ ♆ 9ª ☉ ☌ ♀ 6ₚ ☿ △ ♄ 9ₚ ☾ ☍ ♃ 10ₚ
3	
4	☾ ● ☿ 12ₚ
5	☽ ● ♀ 8ª
5	☽ ☍ ♁ 10ª
7	☿ △ ♂ 1ª
8	
9	☽ ☍ ♂ 2ª
0	
1	☽ ☌ ♇ 5ª

Planet positions in zodiac

☿	Mercury	♍	
♀	Venus	♍ 30 ♎	
♂	Mars	♉	(30 R)
♃	Jupiter	♓	(R)
♄	Saturn	♑	(R 23 D)
♁	Uranus	♈	(R)
♆	Neptune	♓	(R)
♇	Pluto	♐	

Planet (naked eye) visibility

Evening:
Saturn

All night:
Mars, Jupiter

Morning:
Mercury (to Oct 26)

♓ Pisces	♈ Aries	♉ Taurus	♊ Gemini	♋ Cancer	♌ Leo
♍ Virgo	♎ Libra	♏ Scorpio	♐ Sagittarius	♑ Capricorn	♒ Aquarius

Control pests
(see p. 74 for details)

- **Flies:** burn fly papers at Flower times.
- **Slugs:** ash between Oct 17 8ₚ and Oct 19 1ₚ.

Southern hemisphere

Southern Transplanting Time
Oct 29 11ₚ to Nov 12

My notes

My notes

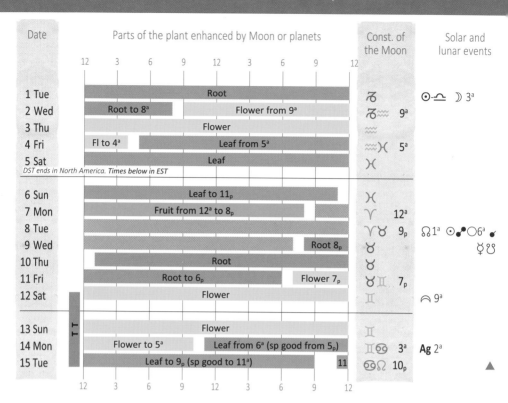

Date	Parts of the plant enhanced by Moon or planets	Const. of the Moon	Solar and lunar events
1 Tue	Root	♐	☉–♎ ☽ 3ᵃ
2 Wed	Root to 8ᵃ / Flower from 9ᵃ	♐♒ 9ᵃ	
3 Thu	Flower	♒	
4 Fri	Fl to 4ᵃ / Leaf from 5ᵃ	♒♓ 5ᵃ	
5 Sat	Leaf	♓	
DST ends in North America. Times below in EST			
6 Sun	Leaf to 11ₚ	♓	
7 Mon	Fruit from 12ᵃ to 8ₚ	♈ 12ᵃ	
8 Tue		♈♉ 9ₚ	☊1ᵃ ☉⚫○6ᵃ
9 Wed	Root 8ₚ	♉	☿☋
10 Thu	Root	♉	
11 Fri	Root to 6ₚ / Flower 7ₚ	♉♊ 7ₚ	
12 Sat	Flower	♊	⌒ 9ᵃ
13 Sun	Flower	♊	
14 Mon	Flower to 5ᵃ / Leaf from 6ᵃ (sp good from 5ₚ)	♊♋ 3ᵃ	**Ag** 2ᵃ
15 Tue	Leaf to 9ₚ (sp good to 11ᵃ) 11	♋♌ 10ₚ	▲

Transplanting Time
(time of descending Moon in northern hemisphere)
Nov 12 11ᵃ to Nov 26 2ᵃ

Leaf times
- Tend leafy plants (like lettuce) during these times.
- Transplant hedges and climbing shrubs during Transplanting Time.

Root times
- Tend root plants (carrots, potatoes) during these times.
- Harvest Jerusalem artichokes, parsnips, leeks.

Fruit times
- Tend fruit plants (beans, grains, tomatoes) during these times.
- **Fruit and forest trees** will benefit from a spraying of horn manure and/or barrel preparation when being transplanted at Fruit times.
- In warm regions harvest table olives.

Flower times
- Tend flowering plants (broccoli, roses) during these times.
- Cut **Advent greenery** and **Christmas trees** for transporting.
- Plant wisterias, begonias and clematis.
- Cut back rose shrubs.
- Sow sweet peas for germinating next spring.

ate   My notes

Planetary aspects
(**Bold** = visible to naked eye)

Planet positions in zodiac

☿	Mercury	♍	4 ♎
			15 ♏
♀	Venus	♎	14 ♏
♂	Mars	♉	(R)
♃	Jupiter	♓	(R)
♄	Saturn	♑	
♅	Uranus	♈	(R)
♆	Neptune	♓	(R)
♇	Pluto	♐	

1 — ☽☌♄ 7ₚ

2 —

3 —

4 — ☽☌♆ 7ᵃ ☽☌♃ 6ₚ

5 — ♀☍☊ 6ₚ

6 —

7 —

8 — ☽☍☿ 6ᵃ ☾●☊ 8ᵃ ☉☌☿ 12ₚ ☾☌♀ 3ₚ ☿☍☊ 10ₚ

9 — ☉☍☊ 3ᵃ ☿☍ 7ᵃ

10 — ♀△♆ 7ᵃ

11 — ☾☌♂ 9ᵃ

12 — ☿△♆ 2ₚ

13 —

14 — ☾☍♇ 1ᵃ ☉△♆ 11ₚ

15 — ♀△♃ 5ᵃ ☾☍♄ 10ₚ

Planet (naked eye) visibility

Evening:
  Saturn

All night:
  Mars, Jupiter

Morning:
  –

♓ Pisces	♈ Aries	♉ Taurus	♊ Gemini	♋ Cancer	♌ Leo
♍ Virgo	♎ Libra	♏ Scorpio	♐ Sagittarius	♑ Capricorn	♒ Aquarius

B: All zodiac symbols refer to astronomical constellations, not astrological signs (see p. 10)

Control pests
(see p. 74 for details)

• **Flies:** burn fly papers at Flower times.

Southern hemisphere

Southern Transplanting Time
Oct 30 to Nov 12 7ᵃ and Nov 26 6ᵃ to Dec 9

Maria Thun's tree log preparations

• Cut **birch** logs, fill with dried **yarrow** and put them into the ground on Nov 5 between 6ᵃ and 11ₚ.

Compost

If not already completed in October, all organic waste materials should be gathered and made into a **compost.** Applying the biodynamic preparations to the compost will ensure a rapid transformation and good fungal development. An application of barrel preparation will also help the composting process.

My notes

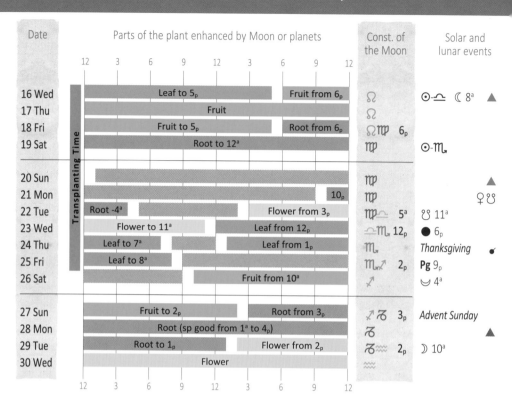

Date	Parts of the plant enhanced by Moon or planets	Const. of the Moon	Solar and lunar events
16 Wed	Leaf to 5ₚ — Fruit from 6ₚ	♌	☉⚎ ☾ 8ᵃ ▲
17 Thu	Fruit	♌	
18 Fri	Fruit to 5ₚ — Root from 6ₚ	♌♍ 6ₚ	
19 Sat	Root to 12ᵃ	♍	☉♏
20 Sun		♍	▲
21 Mon	10ₚ	♍	♀☍
22 Tue	Root -4ᵃ — Flower from 3ₚ	♍⚎ 5ᵃ	☍ 11ᵃ
23 Wed	Flower to 11ᵃ — Leaf from 12ₚ	⚎♏ 12ₚ	● 6ₚ
24 Thu	Leaf to 7ᵃ — Leaf from 1ₚ	♏	*Thanksgiving*
25 Fri	Leaf to 8ᵃ	♏♐ 2ₚ	**Pg** 9ₚ
26 Sat	Fruit from 10ᵃ	♐	☋ 4ᵃ
27 Sun	Fruit to 2ₚ — Root from 3ₚ	♐♑ 3ₚ	*Advent Sunday*
28 Mon	Root (sp good from 1ᵃ to 4ₚ)	♑	▲
29 Tue	Root to 1ₚ — Flower from 2ₚ	♑♒ 2ₚ	☽ 10ᵃ
30 Wed	Flower	♒	

Time scale (top and bottom): 12 3 6 9 12 3 6 9 12

Transplanting Time (vertical label, Nov 16–26)

Transplanting Time
(time of descending Moon in northern hemisphere)
Nov 12 to Nov 26 2ᵃ

Leaf times

- Tend leafy plants (like lettuce) during these times.
- Harvest Brussels sprouts, lettuce, spinach.
- Transplant hedges and climbing shrubs during Transplanting Time.

Root times

- Tend root plants (carrots, potatoes) during these times.

Fruit times

- Tend fruit plants (beans, grains, tomatoes) during these times.
- **Fruit and forest trees** will benefit from a spraying of horn manure and/or barrel preparation when being transplanted at Fruit times.
- Prune fruit trees and shrubs.

Flower times

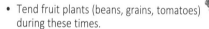

- Tend flowering plants (broccoli, roses) during these times.
- Cut **Advent greenery** and **Christmas trees** for transporting.

ate	My notes	Planetary aspects (**Bold** = visible to naked eye)

Planetary aspects
(**Bold** = visible to naked eye)

Date	Aspects
6	☿△♃ 11ᵃ
7	
8	☾☌♅ 4ₚ
9	☾☍♃ 4ᵃ
0	☉△♃ 11ₚ
1	♀☊ 9ᵃ ☿☌♀ 6ₚ
2	☾☍♅ 4ₚ
3	
4	☽☌♀ 8ᵃ ☽•☿ 10ᵃ
5	☽☍♂ 2ᵃ
6	
7	☽☌♇ 12ₚ
8	♂△♄ 1ₚ
9	☽☌♄ 2ᵃ ☿☍♂ 4ₚ
0	

Planet positions in zodiac

☿	Mercury	♏
♀	Venus	♏
♂	Mars	♉ (R)
♃	Jupiter	♓ (R 23 D)
♄	Saturn	♑
♅	Uranus	♈ (R)
♆	Neptune	♓ (R)
♇	Pluto	♐

Planet (naked eye) visibility

Evening:
Saturn

All night:
Mars, Jupiter

Morning:
–

| ♓ Pisces | ♈ Aries | ♉ Taurus | ♊ Gemini | ♋ Cancer | ♌ Leo |
| ♍ Virgo | ♎ Libra | ♏ Scorpio | ♐ Sagittarius | ♑ Capricorn | ♒ Aquarius |

B: All zodiac symbols refer to astronomical constellations, not astrological signs (see p. 10)

Control pests
(see p. 74 for details)

- **Flies:** burn fly papers at Flower times.

Southern hemisphere

Southern Transplanting Time
Nov 26 6ᵃ to Dec 9

Maria Thun's tree log preparations

- Cut **larch** logs, fill with dried **camomile** and put them into the ground on Nov 29 between 5ᵃ and 10ₚ.

My notes

Compost

If not already completed in October, all organic waste materials should be gathered and made into a **compost**. Applying the biodynamic preparations to the compost will ensure a rapid transformation and good fungal development. An application of barrel preparation will also help the composting process.

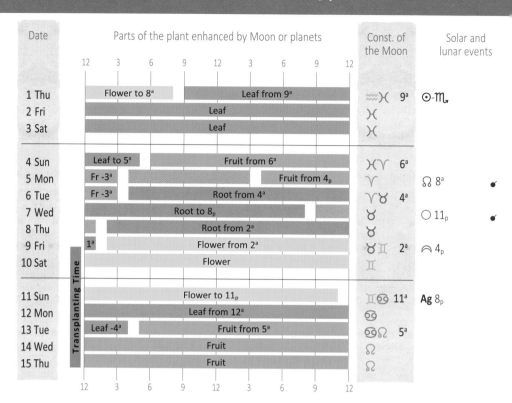

Date	Parts of the plant enhanced by Moon or planets	Const. of the Moon	Solar and lunar events
1 Thu	Flower to 8^a / Leaf from 9^a	♒♓ 9^a	☉-♏
2 Fri	Leaf	♓	
3 Sat	Leaf	♓	
4 Sun	Leaf to 5^a / Fruit from 6^a	♓♈ 6^a	
5 Mon	Fr -3^a / Fruit from 4$_p$	♈	☍ 8^a
6 Tue	Fr -3^a / Root from 4^a	♈♉ 4^a	
7 Wed	Root to 8$_p$	♉	○ 11$_p$
8 Thu	Root from 2^a	♉	
9 Fri	1^a / Flower from 2^a	♉♊ 2^a	⌢ 4$_p$
10 Sat	Flower	♊	
11 Sun	Flower to 11$_p$	♊♋ 11^a	**Ag** 8$_p$
12 Mon	Leaf from 12^a	♋	
13 Tue	Leaf -4^a / Fruit from 5^a	♋♌ 5^a	
14 Wed	Fruit	♌	
15 Thu	Fruit	♌	

Transplanting Time (Dec 9 to Dec 15 shown)

Transplanting Time
(time of descending Moon in northern hemisphere)
Dec 9 6$_p$ to Dec 23 11^a

Fruit times

- Tend fruit plants (beans, grains, tomatoes) during these times.

Leaf times

- Tend leafy plants (like lettuce) during these times.
- On a mild day, prune decidous trees during Transplanting Time.

Flower times

- Tend flowering plants (broccoli, roses) during these times.
- Cut **Advent greenery** and **Christmas trees** to ensure lasting fragrance.

Root times
- Tend root plants (carrots, potatoes) during these times.

Pruning trees and hedges
- Transplanting Time is good for **pruning trees and hedges.** Fruit trees should be pruned at Fruit or Flower times.

te   My notes

Planetary aspects
(**Bold** = visible to naked eye)

♀ ☌ ♂ 1ᵃ   ☽ ☌ ♆ 11ᵃ   ☽ ☌ ♃ 10ₚ

☽ ☍ ⛢ 1ₚ

☽ ☍ ♂ 11ₚ
☉ ☍ ♂ 1ᵃ
☾ ☍ ♀ 1ᵃ   ☾ ☍ ☿ 11ᵃ

☾ ☍ ♇ 9ᵃ

☾ ☍ ♄ 9ᵃ

Planet positions in zodiac

☿	Mercury	♏ 5	♐
♀	Venus	♏ 8	♐
♂	Mars	♉	(R)
♃	Jupiter	♓	
♄	Saturn	♑	
⛢	Uranus	♈	(R)
♆	Neptune	♓	(R 3 D)
♇	Pluto	♐	

Planet (naked eye) visibility

Evening:
Mercury (from Dec 14),
Venus (from Dec 3), Saturn

All night:
Mars, Jupiter

Morning:
—

Pisces	♈ Aries	♉ Taurus	♊ Gemini	♋ Cancer	♌ Leo
Virgo	♎ Libra	♏ Scorpio	♐ Sagittarius	♑ Capricorn	♒ Aquarius

: All zodiac symbols refer to astronomical constellations, not astrological signs (see p. 10)

Control pests
(see p. 74 for details)

- Burn feathers or skins of **warm blooded pests** from Dec 6 4ᵃ to Dec 8 8ₚ. *The burning (and grinding) should be completed by Dec 8 8ₚ.*

My notes

Southern hemisphere

Southern Transplanting Time
Nov 26 to Dec 9 2ₚ and Dec 23 3ₚ to Jan 5

My notes

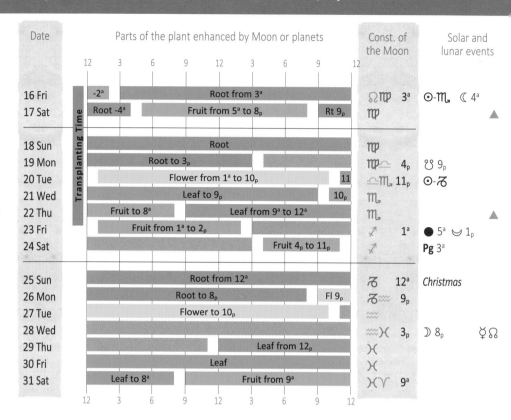

Date	Parts of the plant enhanced by Moon or planets	Const. of the Moon	Solar and lunar events
16 Fri	-2ª Root from 3ª	♌♍ 3ª	☉-♏ ☾ 4ª
17 Sat	Root -4ª Fruit from 5ª to 8ₚ Rt 9ₚ	♍	▲
18 Sun	Root	♍	
19 Mon	Root to 3ₚ	♍♎ 4ₚ	☋ 9ₚ
20 Tue	Flower from 1ª to 10ₚ 11	♎♏ 11ₚ	☉-♑
21 Wed	Leaf to 9ₚ 10ₚ	♏	
22 Thu	Fruit to 8ª Leaf from 9ª to 12ª	♏	▲
23 Fri	Fruit from 1ª to 2ₚ	♐ 1ª	
24 Sat	Fruit 4ₚ to 11ₚ	♐	● 5ª ☋ 1ₚ Pg 3ª
25 Sun	Root from 12ª	♑ 12ª	*Christmas*
26 Mon	Root to 8ₚ Fl 9ₚ	♑ 9ₚ	
27 Tue	Flower to 10ₚ	♒	
28 Wed	Leaf from 12ₚ	♒♓ 3ₚ	☽ 8ₚ ☿♌
29 Thu	Leaf from 12ₚ	♓	
30 Fri	Leaf	♓	
31 Sat	Leaf to 8ª Fruit from 9ª	♓♈ 9ª	

(Left vertical label: Transplanting Time)

Time scale: 12 – 3 – 6 – 9 – 12 – 3 – 6 – 9 – 12

Transplanting Time
(time of descending Moon in northern hemisphere)
Dec 9 to Dec 23 11ª

Leaf times

- Tend leafy plants (like lettuce) during these times.

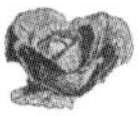

Root times
- Tend root plants (carrots, potatoes) during these times.

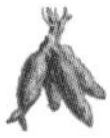

Fruit times
- Tend fruit plants (beans, grains, tomatoes) during these times.

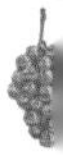

Flower times

- Tend flowering plants (broccoli, roses) during these times.
- Cut **Advent greenery** and **Christmas trees** to ensure lasting fragrance.

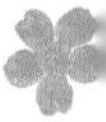

Pruning trees and hedges
- Transplanting Time is good for **pruning trees and hedges.** Fruit trees should be pruned at Fruit or Flower times.

te   My notes   Planetary aspects

(**Bold** = visible to naked eye)

☾☌♇ 1ᵃ   ☾☌♃ 2ₚ

☿△♋ 5ₚ

☾☌♋ 2ᵃ

☾☌♂ 9ₚ

♀△♋ 5ₚ

☽☌♀ 7ᵃ   ☽☌☿ 3ₚ   ☽☌♇ 10ₚ

☽☌♄ 1ₚ

☽☌♆ 5ₚ   ☿☋ 11ₚ

☽☌♃ 7ᵃ   ☿☌♀ 9ᵃ

Planet positions in zodiac

☿ Mercury ♐ (29 R)

♀ Venus ♐

♂ Mars ♉ (R)

♃ Jupiter ♓

♄ Saturn ♑

♅ Uranus ♈ (R)

♆ Neptune ♓

♇ Pluto ♐

Planet (naked eye) visibility

Evening:
Mercury (to Dec 30),
Venus, Jupiter, Saturn

All night:
Mars

Morning:
–

Pisces	♈ Aries	♉ Taurus	♊ Gemini	♋ Cancer	♌ Leo
Virgo	♎ Libra	♏ Scorpio	♐ Sagittarius	♑ Capricorn	♒ Aquarius

My notes

Southern hemisphere

Southern Transplanting Time
Dec 23 3ₚ to Jan 5

My notes

Crop tables

Following tables suggest suitable times for sowing and harvesting particular crops. This makes it easier to find the right calendar page for detailed timings. The times are for northern hemisphere, and may need adjusting to your local climate. Between these times, the plants need tending: thinning out, transplanting, hoeing, weeding, watering, composting or manuring.

- Sow and plant in the greenhouse or under cover, depending on the season and your local climate.
- Transplant during Transplanting Time (descending Moon) at Root, Leaf, Flower or Fruit time as appropriate.
- Tend (hoeing, weeding, watering, composting) and harvest at Root, Leaf, Flower or Fruit time as appropriate.

Root vegetables

Beets

Sow	Jan	Feb	Mar	**April**	**May**	**June**	July	Aug	Sep	Oct	Nov	Dec
Harvest	Jan	Feb	Mar	April	May	June	**July**	**Aug**	**Sep**	**Oct**	Nov	Dec

Carrots

Sow	**Jan**	**Feb**	**Mar**	April	May	June	July	Aug	Sep	Oct	**Nov**	Dec
Harvest	Jan	Feb	Mar	**April**	**May**	**June**	**July**	**Aug**	**Sep**	**Oct**	**Nov**	**Dec**

Celeriac

Sow	Jan	Feb	**Mar**	**April**	**May**	**June**	July	Aug	Sep	Oct	Nov	Dec
Harvest	Jan	Feb	Mar	April	May	**June**	**July**	**Aug**	**Sep**	**Oct**	**Nov**	**Dec**

Garlic

Sow	**Jan**	**Feb**	**Mar**	April	May	June	July	Aug	Sep	**Oct**	**Nov**	**Dec**
Harvest	Jan	Feb	Mar	April	**May**	**June**	**July**	**Aug**	Sep	Oct	Nov	Dec

Horseradish

Sow	Jan	Feb	**Mar**	**April**	**May**	**June**	July	Aug	Sep	Oct	Nov	Dec
Harvest	Jan	Feb	Mar	April	**May**	**June**	**July**	**Aug**	**Sep**	**Oct**	**Nov**	**Dec**

Jerusalem artichoke

Sow	**Jan**	**Feb**	**Mar**	**April**	**May**	June	July	Aug	Sep	Oct	Nov	Dec
Harvest	**Jan**	**Feb**	Mar	April	May	June	July	**Aug**	**Sep**	**Oct**	**Nov**	**Dec**

Onion

Sow	**Jan**	**Feb**	**Mar**	**April**	May	June	July	Aug	Sep	Oct	Nov	Dec
Harvest	Jan	Feb	Mar	April	**May**	**June**	**July**	**Aug**	Sep	Oct	Nov	Dec

Parsnip

	Jan	Feb	Mar	April	May	June	July	Aug	Sep	Oct	Nov	Dec
Sow	Jan	**Feb**	**Mar**	**April**	**May**	**June**	July	Aug	Sep	Oct	Nov	Dec
Harvest	**Jan**	**Feb**	**Mar**	April	May	June	July	Aug	**Sep**	**Oct**	**Nov**	**Dec**

Potato, root tubers

	Jan	Feb	Mar	April	May	June	July	Aug	Sep	Oct	Nov	Dec
Sow	Jan	**Feb**	**Mar**	**April**	May	June	July	Aug	Sep	Oct	Nov	Dec
Harvest	Jan	Feb	Mar	April	**May**	**June**	**July**	**Aug**	**Sep**	Oct	Nov	Dec

Radish

	Jan	Feb	Mar	April	May	June	July	Aug	Sep	Oct	Nov	Dec
Sow	**Jan**	**Feb**	**Mar**	**April**	**May**	**June**	**July**	**Aug**	**Sep**	**Oct**	**Nov**	**Dec**
Harvest	**Jan**	**Feb**	**Mar**	**April**	**May**	**June**	**July**	**Aug**	**Sep**	**Oct**	**Nov**	**Dec**

Salsify

	Jan	Feb	Mar	April	May	June	July	Aug	Sep	Oct	Nov	Dec
Sow	Jan	Feb	**Mar**	**April**	**May**	**June**	**July**	**Aug**	Sep	Oct	Nov	Dec
Harvest	**Jan**	**Feb**	Mar	April	May	June	July	Aug	Sep	**Oct**	**Nov**	**Dec**

Shallots

	Jan	Feb	Mar	April	May	June	July	Aug	Sep	Oct	Nov	Dec
Sow	Jan	Feb	Mar	April	May	June	July	Aug	**Sep**	**Oct**	Nov	Dec
Harvest	Jan	**Feb**	**Mar**	April	May	June	July	Aug	Sep	Oct	Nov	Dec

Leaf plants

Asparagus

	Jan	Feb	Mar	April	May	June	July	Aug	Sep	Oct	Nov	Dec
Sow	**Jan**	**Feb**	**Mar**	**April**	**May**	June	July	Aug	Sep	Oct	Nov	Dec
Harvest	Jan	Feb	**Mar**	**April**	**May**	**June**	**July**	**Aug**	**Sep**	Oct	Nov	Dec

Bok choy *see* Chinese cabbage

Brussels sprouts

	Jan	Feb	Mar	April	May	June	July	Aug	Sep	Oct	Nov	Dec
Sow	Jan	Feb	**Mar**	**April**	**May**	June	July	Aug	Sep	Oct	Nov	Dec
Harvest	**Jan**	**Feb**	**Mar**	April	May	June	July	Aug	**Sep**	**Oct**	**Nov**	**Dec**

Cabbage

	Jan	Feb	Mar	April	May	June	July	Aug	Sep	Oct	Nov	Dec
Sow	**Jan**	**Feb**	**Mar**	**April**	**May**	**June**	**July**	**Aug**	**Sep**	**Oct**	Nov	Dec
Harvest	Jan	Feb	Mar	April	**May**	**June**	**July**	**Aug**	**Sep**	**Oct**	**Nov**	Dec

Celery

	Jan	Feb	Mar	April	May	June	July	Aug	Sep	Oct	Nov	Dec
Sow	Jan	Feb	**Mar**	**April**	**May**	June	July	Aug	Sep	Oct	Nov	Dec
Harvest	Jan	Feb	Mar	April	May	June	July	**Aug**	**Sep**	**Oct**	**Nov**	Dec

Chard

	Jan	Feb	Mar	April	May	June	July	Aug	Sep	Oct	Nov	Dec
Sow	Jan	Feb	Mar	**April**	**May**	**June**	July	Aug	Sep	Oct	Nov	Dec
Harvest	Jan	Feb	Mar	April	May	June	**July**	**Aug**	**Sep**	**Oct**	**Nov**	Dec

Chicory (endives)

	Jan	Feb	Mar	April	May	June	July	Aug	Sep	Oct	Nov	Dec
Sow	Jan	Feb	Mar	April	**May**	**June**	July	Aug	Sep	Oct	Nov	Dec
Harvest	Jan	Feb	Mar	April	May	**June**	**July**	**Aug**	**Sep**	**Oct**	**Nov**	**Dec**

Chinese cabbage (pe-tsai, bok choy)

	Jan	Feb	Mar	April	May	June	July	Aug	Sep	Oct	Nov	Dec
Sow	Jan	Feb	Mar	April	**May**	**June**	**July**	**Aug**	**Sep**	Oct	Nov	Dec
Harvest	Jan	Feb	Mar	April	May	June	July	Aug	**Sep**	**Oct**	**Nov**	**Dec**

Corn salad *see* Lamb's lettuce
Curly kale (green cabbage)

	Jan	Feb	Mar	April	May	June	July	Aug	Sep	Oct	Nov	Dec
Sow	Jan	Feb	Mar	April	May	June	July	Aug	Sep	Oct	Nov	Dec
Harvest	Jan	Feb	Mar	April	May	June	July	Aug	Sep	Oct	Nov	Dec

Endives *see* Chicory
Grass (lawns)

	Jan	Feb	Mar	April	May	June	July	Aug	Sep	Oct	Nov	Dec
Sow	Jan	Feb	Mar	April	May	June	July	Aug	Sep	Oct	Nov	Dec
Mow	Jan	Feb	Mar	April	May	June	July	Aug	Sep	Oct	Nov	Dec

Green cabbage *see* Curly kale
Kohlrabi

	Jan	Feb	Mar	April	May	June	July	Aug	Sep	Oct	Nov	Dec
Sow	Jan	Feb	Mar	April	May	June	July	Aug	Sep	Oct	Nov	Dec
Harvest	Jan	Feb	Mar	April	May	June	July	Aug	Sep	Oct	Nov	Dec

Lamb's lettuce (corn salad)

	Jan	Feb	Mar	April	May	June	July	Aug	Sep	Oct	Nov	Dec
Sow	Jan	Feb	Mar	April	May	June	July	Aug	Sep	Oct	Nov	Dec
Harvest	Jan	Feb	Mar	April	May	June	July	Aug	Sep	Oct	Nov	Dec

Leaf herbs

	Jan	Feb	Mar	April	May	June	July	Aug	Sep	Oct	Nov	Dec
Sow	Jan	Feb	Mar	April	May	June	July	Aug	Sep	Oct	Nov	Dec
Harvest	Jan	Feb	Mar	April	May	June	July	Aug	Sep	Oct	Nov	Dec

Leek

	Jan	Feb	Mar	April	May	June	July	Aug	Sep	Oct	Nov	Dec
Sow	Jan	Feb	Mar	April	May	June	July	Aug	Sep	Oct	Nov	Dec
Harvest	Jan	Feb	Mar	April	May	June	July	Aug	Sep	Oct	Nov	Dec

Lettuce, crisphead (iceberg) lettuce

	Jan	Feb	Mar	April	May	June	July	Aug	Sep	Oct	Nov	Dec
Sow	Jan	Feb	Mar	April	May	June	July	Aug	Sep	Oct	Nov	Dec
Harvest	Jan	Feb	Mar	April	May	June	July	Aug	Sep	Oct	Nov	Dec

Lettuce, winter

	Jan	Feb	Mar	April	May	June	July	Aug	Sep	Oct	Nov	Dec
Sow	Jan	Feb	Mar	April	May	June	July	Aug	Sep	Oct	Nov	Dec
Harvest	Jan	Feb	Mar	April	May	June	July	Aug	Sep	Oct	Nov	Dec

Red cabbage

	Jan	Feb	Mar	April	May	June	July	Aug	Sep	Oct	Nov	Dec
Sow	Jan	Feb	Mar	April	May	June	July	Aug	Sep	Oct	Nov	Dec
Harvest	Jan	Feb	Mar	April	May	June	July	Aug	Sep	Oct	Nov	Dec

Rhubarb

	Jan	Feb	Mar	April	May	June	July	Aug	Sep	Oct	Nov	Dec
Sow	Jan	Feb	Mar	April	May	June	July	Aug	Sep	Oct	Nov	Dec
Harvest	Jan	Feb	Mar	April	May	June	July	Aug	Sep	Oct	Nov	Dec

Spinach

	Jan	Feb	Mar	April	May	June	July	Aug	Sep	Oct	Nov	Dec
Sow	Jan	Feb	Mar	April	May	June	July	Aug	Sep	Oct	Nov	Dec
Harvest	Jan	Feb	Mar	April	May	June	July	Aug	Sep	Oct	Nov	Dec

Flower plants

Artichoke (globe)

	Jan	Feb	Mar	April	May	June	July	Aug	Sep	Oct	Nov	Dec
Sow	Jan	Feb	Mar	April	**May**	June	July	Aug	Sep	Oct	Nov	Dec
Harvest	Jan	Feb	Mar	April	May	June	July	Aug	**Sep**	**Oct**	**Nov**	**Dec**

Broccoli

	Jan	Feb	Mar	April	May	June	July	Aug	Sep	Oct	Nov	Dec
Sow	Jan	**Feb**	**Mar**	**April**	**May**	**June**	**July**	Aug	Sep	Oct	Nov	Dec
Harvest	Jan	Feb	**Mar**	**April**	**May**	**June**	**July**	**Aug**	**Sep**	**Oct**	**Nov**	Dec

Cauliflower

	Jan	Feb	Mar	April	May	June	July	Aug	Sep	Oct	Nov	Dec
Sow	**Jan**	**Feb**	**Mar**	April	May	June	July	Aug	Sep	Oct	Nov	Dec
Harvest	**Jan**	**Feb**	**Mar**	**April**	**May**	**June**	**July**	**Aug**	**Sep**	**Oct**	**Nov**	Dec

Flower bulbs

	Jan	Feb	Mar	April	May	June	July	Aug	Sep	Oct	Nov	Dec
Sow	Jan	Feb	Mar	April	May	June	July	**Aug**	**Sep**	**Oct**	**Nov**	**Dec**
Harvest	Jan	**Feb**	**Mar**	**April**	**May**	June	July	Aug	Sep	Oct	Nov	Dec

Flowers, flowery herbs

	Jan	Feb	Mar	April	May	June	July	Aug	Sep	Oct	Nov	Dec
Sow	Jan	Feb	Mar	April	May	June	July	**Aug**	**Sep**	**Oct**	**Nov**	**Dec**
Harvest	**Jan**	**Feb**	**Mar**	**April**	**May**	**June**	**July**	**Aug**	Sep	Oct	Nov	Dec

Rose

	Jan	Feb	Mar	April	May	June	July	Aug	Sep	Oct	Nov	Dec
Sow	**Jan**	**Feb**	**Mar**	April	May	June	July	Aug	Sep	Oct	**Nov**	**Dec**
Harvest	Jan	Feb	Mar	April	**May**	**June**	**July**	**Aug**	**Sep**	**Oct**	Nov	Dec

Sunflower

	Jan	Feb	Mar	April	May	June	July	Aug	Sep	Oct	Nov	Dec
Sow	Jan	**Feb**	**Mar**	**April**	May	June	July	Aug	Sep	Oct	Nov	Dec
Harvest	Jan	Feb	Mar	April	**May**	**June**	**July**	**Aug**	**Sep**	**Oct**	**Nov**	**Dec**

Fruit plants

Aubergine (eggplant)

	Jan	Feb	Mar	April	May	June	July	Aug	Sep	Oct	Nov	Dec
Sow	**Jan**	**Feb**	**Mar**	April	May	June	July	Aug	Sep	Oct	Nov	Dec
Harvest	Jan	Feb	Mar	April	May	June	**July**	**Aug**	**Sep**	**Oct**	Nov	Dec

Barley *see* Grain

Beans, lentils

	Jan	Feb	Mar	April	May	June	July	Aug	Sep	Oct	Nov	Dec
Sow	Jan	Feb	Mar	April	**May**	**June**	**July**	Aug	Sep	Oct	Nov	Dec
Harvest	Jan	Feb	Mar	April	May	June	**July**	**Aug**	**Sep**	**Oct**	Nov	Dec

Corn *see* Maize

Courgette (zucchini)

	Jan	Feb	Mar	April	May	June	July	Aug	Sep	Oct	Nov	Dec
Sow	Jan	Feb	**Mar**	**April**	**May**	**June**	July	Aug	Sep	Oct	Nov	Dec
Harvest	Jan	Feb	Mar	April	May	**June**	**July**	**Aug**	**Sep**	**Oct**	Nov	Dec

Cucumber

	Jan	Feb	Mar	April	May	June	July	Aug	Sep	Oct	Nov	Dec
Sow	Jan	Feb	**Mar**	**April**	**May**	**June**	July	Aug	Sep	Oct	Nov	Dec
Harvest	Jan	Feb	Mar	April	May	**June**	**July**	**Aug**	**Sep**	**Oct**	Nov	Dec

Eggplant *see* **Aubergine**

Grains (wheat, barley, rye, oats, etc.)

Sow	Jan	Feb	Mar	April	May	**June**	**July**	**Aug**	**Sep**	Oct	Nov	Dec
Harvest	**Jan**	**Feb**	**Mar**	**April**	**May**	June	July	Aug	**Sep**	**Oct**	**Nov**	**Dec**

Maize (corn, sweetcorn)

Sow	Jan	Feb	**Mar**	**April**	**May**	**June**	July	Aug	Sep	Oct	Nov	Dec
Harvest	Jan	Feb	Mar	April	May	June	**July**	**Aug**	**Sep**	**Oct**	**Nov**	**Dec**

Melon

Sow	Jan	**Feb**	**Mar**	**April**	May	June	July	Aug	Sep	Oct	Nov	Dec
Harvest	Jan	Feb	Mar	April	May	June	**July**	**Aug**	**Sep**	Oct	Nov	Dec

Oats *see* **Grain**

Paprika, chilli and sweet pepper

Sow	**Jan**	**Feb**	**Mar**	April	May	June	July	Aug	Sep	Oct	Nov	Dec
Harvest	Jan	Feb	Mar	April	May	June	**July**	**Aug**	**Sep**	**Oct**	Nov	Dec

Pea

Sow	**Jan**	**Feb**	**Mar**	**April**	**May**	June	July	Aug	Sep	**Oct**	**Nov**	**Dec**
Harvest	Jan	Feb	**Mar**	**April**	**May**	**June**	**July**	Aug	Sep	Oct	Nov	Dec

Pumpkin *see* **Squash**

Runner bean (pole bean)

Sow	Jan	Feb	Mar	April	**May**	**June**	**July**	Aug	Sep	Oct	Nov	Dec
Harvest	Jan	Feb	Mar	April	May	June	**July**	**Aug**	**Sep**	**Oct**	Nov	Dec

Rye *see* **Grain**

Soya

Sow	Jan	Feb	Mar	**April**	**May**	**June**	July	Aug	Sep	Oct	Nov	Dec
Harvest	Jan	Feb	Mar	April	**May**	**June**	**July**	**Aug**	**Sep**	**Oct**	**Nov**	**Dec**

Squash (pumpkin)

Sow	Jan	Feb	**Mar**	**April**	**May**	**June**	July	Aug	Sep	Oct	Nov	Dec
Harvest	Jan	Feb	Mar	April	May	**June**	**July**	**Aug**	**Sep**	**Oct**	Nov	Dec

Strawberry

Sow	Jan	Feb	Mar	April	May	June	July	**Aug**	**Sep**	**Oct**	Nov	Dec
Harvest	Jan	Feb	Mar	**April**	**May**	**June**	**July**	**Aug**	**Sep**	Oct	Nov	Dec

Sweetcorn *see* **Maize**

Tomato

Sow	Jan	**Feb**	**Mar**	**April**	May	June	July	Aug	Sep	Oct	Nov	Dec
Harvest	Jan	Feb	Mar	April	May	**June**	**July**	**Aug**	**Sep**	**Oct**	Nov	Dec

Wheat *see* **Grain**

Zucchini *see* **Courgette**

Companion planting

Plants grown in close proximity influence each other, and the technique of companion planting is sometimes used for pest control, pollination or simply maximizing space. For instance, leeks keep away carrot flies and carrots discourage leek moths.

Maria Thun was sceptical about companion planting, as the plants grown together are often different types (leeks are Leaf plants and carrots are Root plants). When trying to enhance their growth through the activity of hoeing and general care of the plants at Leaf or Root times, it is impossible to do justice to both plants. One or the other crop will suffer. Therefore work should be done on prime crops at times that are most beneficial to them.

The following table (based on Philbrick & Gregg, *Companion Plants*) shows which plants help vegetable, fruit, cereal and herb crops to thrive by encouraging growth, deterring pests or preventing disease.

Prime crop
  Companion crops
	Prime crop
	  Companion crops

Apple tree
  chive, nasturtium, vetch, wallflower
	Broccoli (*see also* Cabbage)
	  beetroot (beet), nasturtium

Asparagus
  parsley, tomato
	Cabbage, Brussels sprout, kale
	  beetroot (beet), camomile,

Aubergine (eggplant)
  green (bush) bean
	celery, dill, hyssop, lettuce, mint,
	  potato, rosemary, sage, thyme

Bean (all types)
  beetroot (beet), cabbage, carrot,
  cauliflower, corn (maize),
  cucumber, marigold, potato
	Carrot
	  chive, leek, lettuce, onion, radish,
	  rosemary, sage

Bean, broad (fava)
  corn (maize), oat, potato
	Cauliflower (*see also* Cabbage)
	  celery

Bean, green (bush)
  cabbage, celery, corn (maize),
  cucumber, potato, strawberry,
  summer savory
	Celeriac
	  leek

Bean, runner (pole)
  corn (maize), radish
	Celery
	  green (bush) bean, leek, onion
	  tomato

Beets, beetroot
  cabbage, green (bush) bean,
  lettuce, kohlrabi, onion
	Chervil
	  radish, yarrow

	Citrus tree
	  guava, live (evergreen) oak,
	  rubber tree

Prime crop
   Companion crops
	Prime crop
	   Companion crops

Corn (maize)
  bean, cucumber, pea, potato,
  wheat
	Potato
	  bean (except butter bean/
	  lima), cabbage, corn, dead nettle
	  (henbit), flax, horseradish,
	  marigold, nasturtium, pea,
	  sainfoin (esparcet)

Cucumber
  cabbage, celeriac, corn, green
  (bush) bean, kohlrabi, lettuce,
  potato, radish, sunflower	

Fruit tree
  chive, garlic, horseradish,
  legumes, mustard, nasturtium,
  stinging nettle, tansy, vetch
	Radish
	  chervil, lettuce, kohlrabi,
	  nasturtium, pea, runner (pole)
	  bean

Garlic
  rose
	Rosemary
	  sage, yarrow

Grapevine
  elm tree, hyssop, legumes,
  mulberry, mustard
	Rye
	  pansy, vetch

Herbs
  stinging nettle, yarrow
	Sage
	  rosemary, yarrow

Kale *see* Cabbage	**Spinach** strawberry

Kohlrabi *(see also* Cabbage)
  beetroot (beet), lettuce, onion
	Squash (pumpkin)
	  corn (maize), nasturtium

Leek
  carrot, celeriac, celery
	Strawberry
	  borage, green (bush) bean,
	  lettuce, spinach

Lettuce
  beetroot (beet), cabbage,
  camomile, carrot, strawberry
	Tomato
	  asparagus, celery, marigold,
	  parsley, stinging nettle

Melon
  corn (maize)
	Turnip, swede (rutabaga)
	  pea

Oat
  vetch
	Wheat
	  corn (maize), sainfoin (esparcet)

Onion
  beetroot (beet), carrot, celery,
  lettuce, summer savory	

Pea
  bean, carrot, cucumber, radish,
  potato, corn (maize), turnip/
  swede (rutabaga)
	Border plants that benefit **most
	vegetables:** bean, borage, camomile,
	chervil, chive, dead nettle (henbit),
	dill, lavender, hyssop, lovage,
	marjoram, parsley, pea, sage,

Peach tree tansy	sainfoin (esparcet), tarragon, thyme, valerian, hyssop, lemon balm, yarrow (not fennel or wormwood)

Biodynamic preparations

The compost preparations

The classic preparation plants used by biodynamic practitioners for compost preparations are picked, dried and inserted into animal sheaths (skull, bladder, etc.). For more see Further Reading, p. 95.

- Pick *dandelions* in the morning at Flower times as soon as they are open, while the centre of the flowers are still tightly packed.
- Pick *yarrow* at Fruit times when the Sun is in Leo (around the middle of August).
- Pick *camomile* at Flower times just before midsummer. If they are harvested too late, seeds will begin to form and there are often grubs in the hollow heads.
- Collect *stinging nettles* when the first flowers are opening, usually around midsummer. Harvest the whole plants without roots at Flower times.
- Pick *valerian* at Flower times around midsummer.
- Collect *oak bark* at Root times. The pithy material below the bark should not be used.

All the flowers (except valerian) should be laid out on paper and dried in the shade.

Maria Thun's tree log preparations

Many of the classic biodynamic preparations require the use of animal organs. With the onset of BSE, using them became more difficult. This led Maria Thun to develop preparations using the bark of trees instead. They are not counted among the biodynamic preparations developed by Rudolf Steiner, but they do build on indications gained through his approach and can be used in biodynamic agriculture.

The plants should be picked and dried as indicated above. The logs for the bark need to be cut, filled and buried in the ground in accordance with lunar and planetary rhythms. These times (indicated in the almanac) need to be kept with some precision otherwise the preparations may be less effective. Since these planetary constellations do not occur regularly and in some years do not arise at all, it is worth making sufficient preparations to last more than one year. They should be stored like all biodynamic preparations, in pots surrounded by peat.

The spray preparations

There are two spray preparations – horn manure and horn silica. Maria Thun's research showed the best times to apply these.

Horn manure is most effective when sprayed on the soil, not on the plants, and is applied three times: before sowing, during sowing and after sowing. Its effect is to help the seeds and young seedlings to orientate themselves better in the soil.

Horn silica is best sprayed at Fruit times on crops beginning to shoot and form ears. Its effect is to enhance the vitality of the plant. Like horn manure, it must be stirred for a whole hour but is then only effective for up to four hours. This means that it must be sprayed out as soon as possible after stirring. The best time for spraying is immediately after sunrise, so that entails an early start.

Animal and insect pests, fungal problems

When dealing with the often significant issue of animal or insect pests, there is generally no need to reach for biological and chemical pesticides. The first step is to familiarize yourself with the conditions and habits of the pest, and to rectify any management errors that have been made. If despite this, the pest continues, it can be contained within its natural limits by using the ashes of its own burnt remains.

Snails and slugs

For an average infestation, collect between fifty and sixty animals. When the Moon is in Cancer put them in a bucket of water filled to the brim with a close fitting lid. Let it stand for four weeks until the Moon is again in Cancer, then spray the liquid where slugs and snails are a problem. Where slugs and snails are a huge problem, add some

One species, the Great Grey or Leopard Slug (Limex maximus) should be encouraged, as it feeds primarily on decaying plant remains and on the eggs of other slugs. This rare slug is 4 to 7 in (10–18 cm) long and unlike other large brown slugs, it is only active at night.

twenty slugs are to the horn silica preparation and stir it for an hour before spraying over the affected ground where slugs and snails are wont to feed. The light effect of silica is very disagreeable to slugs. Spray three times successively.

Mice, other mammals, birds and insects

Take a few skins of mammals, a few bird feathers, or for insects take 50 or 60 insects. Burn them in a wood fire (don't use grilling charcoal) during the appropriate planetary aspect, indicated in the 'Control pests' notes on the calendar pages. Ensure the fire is glowing hot. Lay dry feathers, skins or dead pests on the embers. After they have cooled, collect the light grey ash and grind for an hour with a pestle and mortar, as this increases its efficacy. The burning and grinding should be completed within the time indicated under Pest Control.

The ashes can be kept in an airtight jar until you need them. Label the jar with type of ash, potency and date.

The ground-up ash can then be potentized (diluted) later.

To make a liquid for spraying, place one gram (or level teaspoon) of this ground-up ash in a small bottle with 9 ml (grams, or teaspoons) of water and shake vigorously for three minutes. This is the first decimal potency (D1 or X1). Add a further 90 ml of water and shake again for three minutes. This is the second decimal potency, D2 or X2. Repeating this procedure until D8 (X8) would produce 100,000 litres (26,000 gallons). It is therefore advisable to proceed until D4 and then start again using smaller quantities (always diluting in the ratio of 1 to 9).

Alternatively the ground-up ash can be diluted with pure wood ash to make a dry ash 'pepper' for spreading on the affected area. Instead of diluting and shaking with water, use wood ash in the same proportions as water above, to make a D8 potency.

Burning skins in a wood oven

Burning in the field

Grinding the ash

Apply the liquid version as a fine mist for three evenings in succession, either using a backpack sprayer, or for large areas using a tractor-mounted sprayer. For the dry version a simple peppershaker can be used for very small areas. For larger areas, use a sowing machine with a piece of rolled-up paper set in the machine to ensure that only a minute amount of ash is released at a time).

Maria Thun advised the D8 potency was as effective as the undiluted ground-up ash, but had the advantage that a far larger area could be treated. In comparative farm trials, in both cases the animal pests remained away from the cultivated fields. The effect of deer ash could be clearly observed on an unfenced clover field where the deer had grazed the clover in the surrounding fields but not within 7 feet (2 m) of the trial area.

Where pests occur in large numbers good results are obtained by burning them on the site where they have been found. Flea beetle and apple blossom weevil can be caught with fly papers for example and burnt on site.

Fungal problems

The function of fungus in nature is to break down dying organic materials. It appears amongst our crops when unripe manure compost or uncomposted animal by-products such as horn and bone meal are used, but also when seeds are harvested during unfavourable constellations: according to Steiner, 'When Moon forces are working too strongly on the Earth.'

Tea can be made from horsetail (*Equisetum arvense*) and sprayed on to the soil where affected plants are growing. This draws the fungal level back down into the ground where it belongs.

The plants can be strengthened by spraying stinging nettle tea on the leaves. This will promote good assimilation, stimulate the flow of sap and help fungal diseases to disappear.

Sowing and felling times for trees and shrubs

Sowing times

We can calculate optimal times for sowing seeds by looking at the Moon's position in the zodiac, depending on the part of the tree or shrub to be enhanced. You can use this method for any trees and shrubs not mentioned here. Sowing times shown here depend on planetary aspects that encourage vitality of the species; they are not specific to either northern or southern hemispheres or to any climatic region. Avoid unfavourable times.

Note: sowing times are different from Transplanting Times. Seedlings should be transplanted during the descending Moon (also called Transplanting Time) when the Moon is in a constellation corresponding to the part of the tree to to be enhanced. It is important to remember that seedlings need to be sufficiently mature to withstand the winter. The time of sowing should therefore be adapted to local conditions and take account of the germination habit of each tree species.

Alder, **Apricot,** *Elm,* **Larch, Peach:**
  July 17 4_p to July 18 9^a
  July 30 3_p to July 31 8^a
  Aug 20 5_p to Aug 21 10^a *(also Magnolia)*
  Sep 2 11^a to Sep 3 4^a
  Sep 18 8^a to Sep 19 1^a
  Oct 12 5^a to 9^a
  Nov 29 5^a to 10_p.

Apple, **Apricot,** *Copper beech, Damson, Maple, Olive,* **Peach, Sweet chestnut,** *Walnut:*
  Sep 2 11^a to Sep 3 4^a
  Sep 18 8^a to Sep 19 1^a
  Sep 26 4^a to 9_p
  Oct 12 5^a to 9^a.

Ash, **Cedar,** *Fir, Hazel,* **Mirabelle plum,** *Rowan,* **Spruce:**
  July 19 10^a to July 20 3^a
  Aug 14 2^a to 7_p *(also Hawthorn)*
  Sep 16 7^a to 11_p
  Sep 26 4^a to 9_p
  Dec 7 2_p to 8_p & Dec 8 2^a to 7^a.

Beech, **Cedar,** *Fir, Hornbeam, Juniper, Palm, Pine, Plum, Quince, Sloe,* **Spruce,** *Thuja:*
  July 30 3_p to July 31 8^a
  Aug 14 2^a to 7_p
  Aug 28 3^a to 8_p.

Birch, **Larch,** *Lime tree,* **Mirabelle plum,** *Pear, Robinia, Willow:*
  Aug 8 2_p to Aug 9 7^a
  Aug 28 3^a to 8_p
  Sep 23 6_p to Sep 24 11^a *(also Magnolia);*
  Nov 5 7^a to 11_p
  Nov 30 1_p to Dec 1 6^a.

Blackcurrant:
  Nov 5 7^a to 11_p.

Cherry, Chestnut, Horse chestnut (Buckeye), Oak, **Sweet chestnut,** *Yew:*
  Nov 29 5^a to 10_p
  Nov 30 1_p to Dec 1 6^a
  Dec 7 2_p to 8_p & Dec 8 2^a to 7^a.

Lilac, Poplar, Sallow, Snowberry:
  Nov 5 7^a to 11_p.

Note: some species (marked in **bold**) appear in two groups.

Felling times

The quality and durability of cut timber can be affected by the felling time. The dates below show optimum times for different groups of trees.

If a large number of these trees need to be felled in a short time, use the time indicated to cut the bark all around the trunk to stop sap flow. The actual felling can be done later.

Trees which are not listed should be felled at the end of the growing season at Flower times. Avoid unfavourable times.

Note that some species (marked in **bold**) appear in two groups.

*Alder, **Apricot**, Elm, **Larch, Peach**:*
  April 28 2^a to 11^a
  May 25 12_p to 11_p
  June 10 11^a to 8_p
  July 2 1^a to 10^a
  July 16 10_p to July 17 7^a *(also Magnolia);*
  July 23 2^a to 8_p
  Aug 16 3^a to 5_p
  Aug 22 12_p to 9_p
  Sep 27 3^a to 12_p
  Oct 6 6_p to Oct 7 3^a
  Oct 22 3_p to 11_p
  Oct 26 12_p to Oct 27 3^a
  Nov 12 8^a to 5_p *(also Magnolia)*
  Nov 15 11_p to Nov 16 5_p
  Dec 17 11^a to 8_p.

*Apple, **Apricot**, Copper beech, Damson, Maple, Olive, **Peach**, **Sweet chestnut**, Walnut:*
  July 23 2^a to 8_p
  July 31 6^a to 12_p
  Aug 17 4_p to Aug 18 2^a
  Nov 14 5_p to Nov 15 11^a
  Nov 15 11_p to Nov 16 5_p.

*Ash, **Cedar, Fir**, Hazel, **Mirabelle plum**, Rowan, **Spruce**:*
  May 19 2^a to 11^a
  June 15 9_p to June 16 6^a;
  July 17 1_p to 10_p
  July 31 6^a to 12_p
  Sep 11 3^a to 12_p
  Sep 18 6_p to Sep 19 3^a
  Oct 17 6^a to 9_p
  Nov 14 5_p to Nov 15 2^a.

*Beech, **Cedar, Fir**, Hornbeam, Juniper, Palm, Pine, Plum, Quince, Spruce, Thuja:*
  June 15 9_p to June 16 6^a;
  July 2 1^a to 10^a
  Sep 27 8_p to Sep 28 5^a
  Oct 13 7_p to Oct 14 5^a
  Oct 22 3_p to 11_p
  Nov 28 1^a to 4_p.

*Birch, **Larch**, Lime tree, **Mirabelle plum**, Pear, Robinia, Willow:*
  June 20 9_p to June 21 7^a
  Aug 7 6^a to 4_p *(also Magnolia)*
  Aug 17 4_p to Aug 18 2^a
  Sep 19 6_p to Sep 20 4^a
  Sep 25 7_p to Sep 26 5^a;
  Oct 13 7_p to Oct 14 5^a
  Nov 10 1^a to 10^a *(also Magnolia)*
  Nov 14 5_p to Nov 15 11^a
  Dec 21 10_p to Dec 22 8^a.

*Cherry, Chestnut, Horse chestnut (Buckeye), Oak, **Sweet chestnut**, Yew:*
  Feb 7 10_p to Feb 8 1_p
  Aug 14 5^a to 8_p
  Sep 27 8_p to Sep 28 5^a
  Oct 17 6^a to 9_p
  Oct 26 12_p to Oct 27 3^a
  Nov 28 1^a to 4_p.

Poplar, Sallow:
  Aug 16 3^a to 5_p
  Sep 19 6_p to Sep 20 4^a
  Dec 17 11^a to 8_p
  Dec 21 10_p to Dec 22 8^a.

Beekeeping

Bees are also influenced by the movement of the Moon. By opening and closing the beehive or skep in rhythm with the Moon, the beekeeper can directly affect the bees' activity. A beekeeping panel is shown on relevant calendar pages.

Constellation	Sign	Element (Type)	Bees	Weather tendency
Pisces	♓	Water (Leaf)	Making honey	Damp
Aries	♈	Warmth (Fruit)	Gathering nectar	Warm/hot
Taurus	♉	Earth (Root)	Building comb	Cool/cold
Gemini	♊	Light (Flower)	Gathering pollen	Airy/bright
Cancer	♋	Water (Leaf)	Making honey	Damp
Leo	♌	Warmth (Fruit)	Gathering nectar	Warm/hot
Virgo	♍	Earth (Root)	Building comb	Cool/cold
Libra	♎	Light (Flower)	Gathering pollen	Airy/bright
Scorpio	♏	Water (Leaf)	Making honey	Damp
Sagittarius	♐	Warmth (Fruit)	Gathering nectar	Warm/hot
Capricorn	♑	Earth (Root)	Building comb	Cool/cold
Aquarius	♒	Light (Flower)	Gathering pollen	Airy/bright

The care of bees

A colony of bees lives in its hive closed off from the outside world. For extra protection against harmful influences, the inside of the hive is sealed with propolis. The link with the wider surroundings is made by the bees that fly in and out of the hive.

To make good use of cosmic rhythms, the beekeeper needs to create the right conditions in much the same way as the gardener or farmer does with the plants. The gardener works the soil and in so doing allows cosmic forces to penetrate it via the air. These forces can then be taken up and used by the plants until the soil is next moved.

When the beekeeper opens up the hive, the sealing layer of propolis is broken. This creates a disturbance, as a result of which lunar and planetary forces can influence the life of the hive until the next intervention by the beekeeper. By this means the beekeeper can directly mediate cosmic forces to the bees.

It is not insignificant which forces of the universe are brought into play when the hive is opened. The beekeeper can consciously intervene by choosing days for working with the hive that will help the colony to develop and build up its food reserves. The bees will then reward the beekeeper by providing a portion of their harvest in the form of honey.

- *Earth-Root* times can be selected for opening the hive if the bees need to do more building.
- *Light-Flower* times encourage brood activity and colony development.
- *Warmth-Fruit* times stimulate the collection of nectar.
- *Water-Leaf* times are unsuitable for working in the hive or for the removal and processing of honey.

Varroa

Since the late 1970s the varroa mite has affected virtually every bee colony in Europe. Following a number of comparative trials Maria Thun recommend burning and making an ash of the varroa mite (as described on pp. 74f). After dynamizing it for one hour, the ash should be put in a salt cellar and sprinkled lightly between the combs. The ash should be made and sprinkled when the Sun and Moon are in Taurus (May/June).

To strengthen the brood, small amounts of ash can also be sprinkled on the brood whenever an inspection is carried out .

Spraying the varroa ash using a salt cellar

Further reading

Berrevoets, Erik, *Wisdom of Bees: Principles of Biodynamic Beekeeping*, SteinerBooks, USA

Colquhoun, Margaret and Axel Ewald, *New Eyes for Plants*, Hawthorn

Karlsson, Britt and Per, *Biodynamic, Organic and Natural Winemaking*, Floris

Keyserlink, Adalbert Count von, *The Birth of a New Agriculture*, Temple Lodge

—, *Developing Biodynamic Agriculture*, Temple Lodge

Klett, Manfred, *Principles of Biodynamic Spray and Compost Preparations*, Floris

Klocek, Dennis, *Sacred Agriculture: The Alchemy of Biodynamics*, Lindisfarne

Koepf, H.H., *The Biodynamic Farm: Agriculture in the Service of Humanity*, SteinerBooks, USA

—, *Koepf's Practical Biodynamics: Soil, Compost, Sprays and Food Quality*, Floris

König, Karl, *Social Farming: Healing Humanity and the Earth*, Floris

Kranich, Ernst Michael, *Planetary Influences upon Plants*, Biodynamic Association, USA

Lepetit, Antoine, *What's so Special About Biodynamic Wine?* Floris

Masson, Pierre, *A Biodynamic Manual*, Floris

Morrow, Joel, *Vegetable Gardening for Organic and Biodynamic Growers*, Lindisfarne

Osthaus, K.-E., *The Biodynamic Farm*, Floris

Pfeiffer, Ehrenfried, *The Earth's Face*, Lanthorn

—, *Pfeiffer's Introduction to Biodynamics*, Floris

—, *Weeds and What They Tell Us*, Floris

—, & Michael Maltas, *The Biodynamic Orchard Book*, Floris

Philbrick, John and Helen, *Gardening for Health and Nutrition*, Anthroposophic, USA

Philbrick, Helen & Gregg, Richard B., *Companion Plants: An A to Z for Gardeners and Farmers*, Floris

Sattler, Friedrich & Eckard von Wistinghausen, *Growing Biodynamic Crops*, Floris

Selg, Peter, *The Agricultural Course: Rudolf Steiner and the Beginnings of Biodynamics*, Temple Lodge

Steiner, Rudolf, *Agriculture (A Course of Eight Lectures)*, Biodynamic Association, USA (also published in another translation by Rudolf Steineer Press, UK)

—, *Agriculture: An Introductory Reader*, Steiner Press, UK

—, *What is Biodynamics? A Way to Heal and Revitalize the Earth*, SteinerBooks, USA

Storl, Wolf, *Culture and Horticulture*, North Atlantic Books, USA

Thun, Maria, *Gardening for Life*, Hawthorn

—, *The Biodynamic Year*, Temple Lodge

Thun, Matthias, *Biodynamic Beekeeping*, Floris

Weiler, Michael, *The Secret of Bees: An Insider's Guide to the Life of the Honeybee*, Floris

Wright, Hilary, *Biodynamic Gardening for Health and Taste*, Floris

Biodynamic associations

Demeter International
www.demeter.net

Australia:
Australian Demeter Bio-Dynamic
demeterbiodynamic.com.au/
Biodynamic Agriculture Australia
www.biodynamics.net.au

Canada (Ontario): Society for Bio-Dynamic Farming & Gardening in Ontario
biodynamics.on.ca (see also USA)

India: Bio-Dynamic Association of India (BDAI)
www.biodynamics.in

Ireland: Biodynamic Agriculture Association of Ireland
www.biodynamicagriculture.ie

New Zealand:
NZ Biodynamic Association
www.biodynamic.org.nz

South Africa: Biodynamic Agricultural Association of Southern Africa
www.bdaasa.org.za

UK: Biodynamic Association
www.biodynamic.org.uk

USA: Biodynamic Assoc. of North America
www.biodynamics.com

Moon diagrams

The diagrams overleaf show for each month the daily position (evenings GMT) of the Moon against the stars and other planets. For viewing in the southern hemisphere, turn the diagrams upside down.

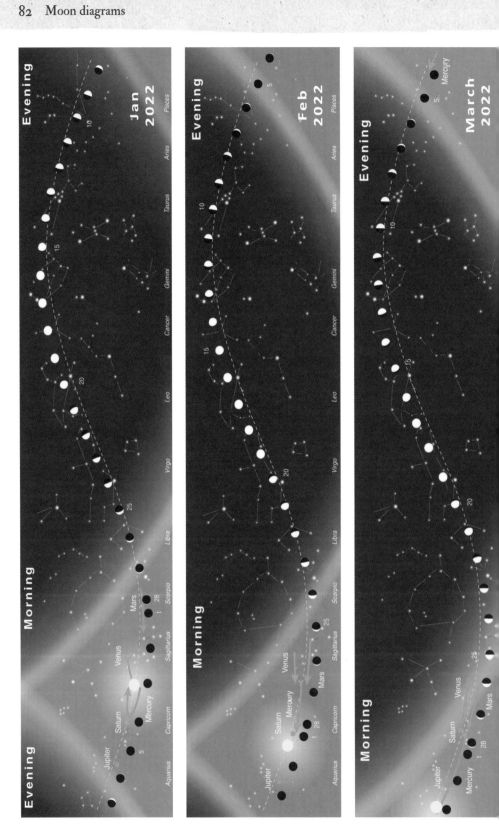

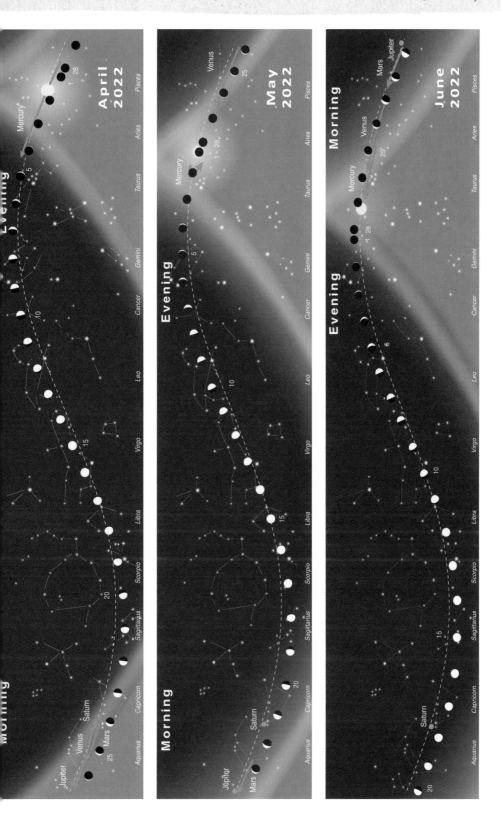

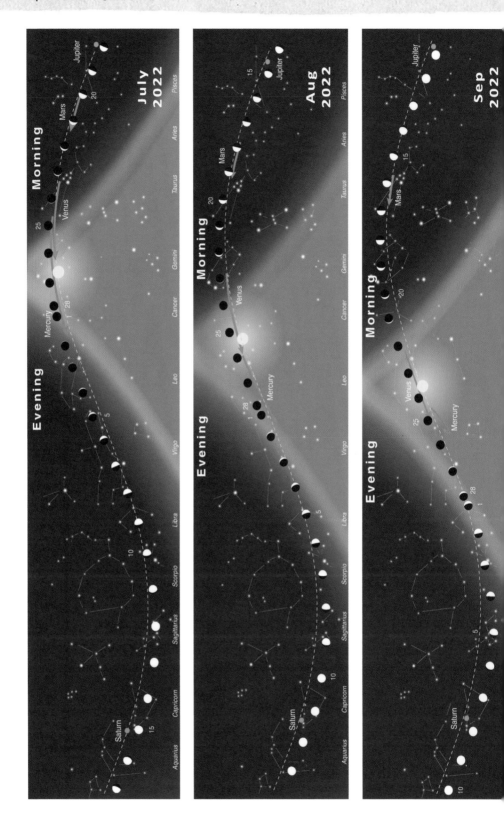

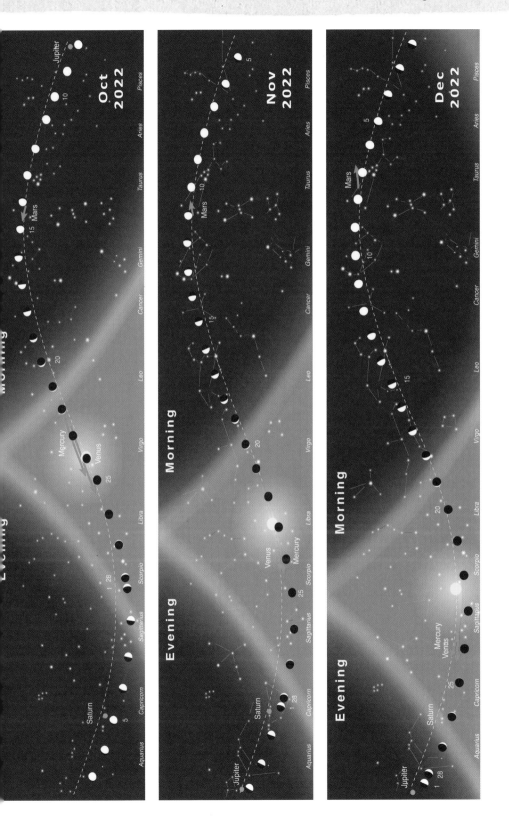

In memory of Matthias Thun

Titia Thun

On June 22, 2020, our dear father, Matthias Kaspar Thun, passed away quite unexpectedly.

At 72 he might not have been a young man, but he was still full of life. He enjoyed watching my brother, Friedrich, take over the farm here in Dexbach and supported him with all his power in this endeavour. In his last year he was able to find pleasure in new animals here, revived many old friendships, finally put down old arguments and also rekindled his relationship to nature with a new passion. His sudden death was therefore a surprise and a shock for us.

Matthias was born in Marburg, Germany, on Sunday February 29, 1948. Again and again he proudly told us that only children who are born on this date of a leap year, and also on a Sunday, are able to find treasure. According to local legend only they are given the gift to see the golden spinning wheel in the River Lahn. Matthias may not have found exactly this spinning wheel, but he was convinced that he had led a lucky life.

He dedicated most of his life to his mother's service, tending her agricultural research and supporting her with heart and soul. Without his support, she would not have been able to carry out her research and maintain a close contact with people around the world who also felt the importance of understanding how cosmic forces worked on earth. He felt obliged to continue publishing the *Maria Thun Biodynamic Almanac* after his mother died, to maintain and continue her work. When she fell ill he cared for her to the end, as he had cared for his father before. He kept the promise he had made to his parents that they could always live and grow old with him.

My brother and I never made such a promise, and we knew we were free to do whatever we wanted to do. My brother Friedrich went into agriculture of his own accord and I made writing my vocation. However, we have been actively working with our father over the past few years, calculating the data and writing for the almanac.

We shall continue the publishing activity and we are ready to take on the task of honouring our grandmother's legacy in this way.

Friedrich (born in 1996) and I (born a year later) are both still comparatively young and even if we tried, we will of course not have the same experience that our father and our grandmother brought to the almanac. Nonetheless, Maria Thun's work will remain at the centre of this almanac – there are countless unpublished texts she wrote that will be reviewed over the coming few years. We will take up the questions that Maria Thun left us and continue to try to answer them.

Maria and Matthias Thun

Horn silica
Maria Thun

Ever since biodynamic farming has existed efforts have been made to understand the observed effects of the preparations. To find out where changes occur when the preparations are applied we must set up comparative trials. We can then see by starting from the phenomena, whether plants treated with the preparations show differences in terms of form, leaf shape or in other ways as compared to untreated plants growing under identical conditions. Some plants are more suited to this task than others. A plant that has the capacity to express significant changes in leaf form will also be capable of showing other differences – unlike grasses and cereals, for instance.

Cereals on the other hand *are* able to show variation in other areas. The form of their ears, the color of their flowers and, in the case of follow-up cultivation, the color of the germinating seedling. Comparisons made within the plant family can reveal more vigorous growth or at other times a reduction in vitality. If a plant is removed from the earth further information can be gleaned from the roots.

Our observations are always based on the phenomena. Another step towards understanding the effects of the preparations can be taken by using size, number and weight to confirm the differences. But this focus on quantity (higher yields) ignores the question of quality. What is quality? How can quality be measured? Simply looking healthy is not enough.

This brings us to the question of the substances contained in the plant. Are we now finally in the realm of quality or still occupied with quantity when we discover a particularly high protein or sugar content? This demonstrates the need to further unpack the concept of quality.

The plant expresses two dominant gestures – one is providing food and the other is producing seed. According to the indications given by Rudolf Steiner in the Agriculture Course, these two tendencies are the consequence of planetary effects. Food quality is enhanced when the Sun's influence is moderated by the working of Mars, Jupiter and Saturn, while Moon, Mercury and Venus enhance the reproductive power. The key question for us is, how we can stimulate the one or the other?

When taken in as food, each part of the plant influences a different area of the human being. The main substances in food are proteins, fats, carbohydrates and salts. These substances arise from life processes and are carriers of invisible forces and processes. However, they leave traces in the substances, and we can try to orientate ourselves via these traces.

When discussing the compost preparations during the Agriculture Course, Rudolf Steiner said that their effect is to enable soil and plants to take up cosmic influences more strongly. He described the subtle influences that stream from the surroundings into the soil and become available to plants. They always change whenever the soil is moved – as the extensive research into different sowing times has confirmed.

Our research into the silica (quartz) preparation shows that the connection between plant and cosmos is strengthened through the application of horn silica.

The daily rhythm

The day has a natural rhythm, which starts with an ascending period during the morning when the light grows stronger. Around midday it reaches a peak as though holding its breath. Then it declines in the afternoon. We can observe a similar activity in plants with ascending forces and rising sap in the morning. Around the hours of noon the plant does not wish to be disturbed and then in the afternoon there is a descending process. Just as in the morning the gesture is one of opening up to the cosmos followed by a kind midday sleep, in the afternoon a stronger connection with the earth is sought.

We have repeatedly observed in our trials how a morning application of the horn silica preparation strongly stimulates the upper part of the plant and the forming of substances, while an afternoon application influences root growth and encourages the fruiting process in the roots. This expresses itself with increased yields but also in changes of root form. For example, in the case of field beans we have often seen how a morning spray enhances the vertical growth tendency while an afternoon spray stimulates the root to develop more of a ball-shape which in turn expresses a fruit-forming tendency.

The plant needs to tune into the changing relationship of the Sun to the Earth during the course of the day, and this is strengthened when horn silica is applied. But this also means that an afternoon application will have a devitalizing effect on the upper part of the plant and it is important to assess whether the plant can cope with such stress during that stage of growth. A morning application always enhances vitality.

If we have grain crop that is ripening too slowly and we give a morning application of horn silica, new vitalizing processes are activated, which might lead to the grain sprouting in the ear. In this case it would be better to apply horn silica in the afternoon to reduce vitality. For root plants (like carrots or potatoes) we must make sure they develop enough foliage for good assimilation. Horn silica should then be applied in the morning during the early growth stages. Only once the plant above ground is fully developed should we give an afternoon spray to enhance the fruiting roots.

The monthly rhythm

With horn silica we found that not only could we enhance the effects of the daily rhythm, but also the rhythm of the Moon's passage through the zodiac, which also influences plant growth. Spraying trials showed how zodiacal influences were enhanced by the silica preparation.

We found that the effect was strongest when the spraying was carried out for:

- root crops at Root times
- leaf crops at Leaf times
- fruit crops at Fruit times

Taking account of the Moon's course through the zodiac when spraying horn silica led to an increase in yield, improved health, better germination and more vigorous seedlings. Subsequent analysis gave strong confirmation of this. Plants treated with horn silica at the right moment were often found to contain more of the trace elements required by human beings. But there were also other improvements – an improved ratio between nitrogen and sugar in spinach leaves or a more favourable protein-carbohydrate ratio in cereal grains. With roots grown for human food it is important to have the right proportion of vegetable salts and here too the best results occur when the application is made under the most favourable cosmic conditions.

Comparative spraying trials with horn silica

How often and at what time of day should we spray horn silica?

The practical question is often raised: how often should horn silica be sprayed to achieve maximum effect? Comparative trials with up to ten successive daily applications have shown that the greatest effect occurs with three or four applications. Further sprayings have no measurable effect.

Numerous trials using different rhythms on various crops have been undertaken with horn silica for more than ten years and the results described above have been confirmed time and again. Analysis of crops using visual image methods (crystallization, chromatograms, water drop pictures) always show the presence of strong formative forces in the plant whenever horn silica had been applied. Storage tests have shown improved keeping quality.

In the case of the four cosmic influences we found that the effects of spraying at Root, Leaf, Fruit or Flower times enhanced the development of that part of the plant.

However, the effect of the silica preparation was diminished in some cases. Plants sown at Flower times and sprayed with the preparation the same day produced lower yields and revealed a hardening tendency in the visual image tests. When their seeds were sown the following year these plants again had lower yields than the control. This seemed to be a question of light. Flower times tend to have an intensive light quality. An hour after spraying, plants often turn the upper surfaces of their leaves away from the light.

At this point we must again look more closely at the time of day when the spraying took place. The reactions of the plants referred to above could, in some cases, also be observed if spraying was carried between noon and 2 pm. To determine the best time of day more precisely, spraying trials were carried out at hourly intervals from dawn till dusk. These showed that the best time for a morning application was before 9 am, and for an afternoon spray after 5 pm. These trials were carried out during long summer days.

This shows that the time of day when the Sun is at its highest is unsuitable for spraying horn silica. Applications carried out at Flower times before 7 am and after 7 pm – when the Sun is low – displayed none of the problems indicated above. It is clear that the preparation has a powerful light effect which the plant is unable to deal with when the external light is at its strongest.

Other trials clearly show that treating plants growing in the shade with the silica preparation enables them to overcome or reduce the effects of shade. Dr Heintz at the University of Strasbourg, who developed a method to show the light effect of the horn silica, has since confirmed the results that we observed in plants.

Stirring the preparation

It was uncertain how long the stirred preparation remains effective. We found through our planting trials that it works for four hours and then gradually loses its effectiveness. Dr Heintz observed something similar. He compared the horn silica preparation with a similar amount of unprepared ground-up quartz and found that the light effect of horn silica was stronger and lasted longer than the ground-up quartz.

This brings us back to the starting substance. For making horn silica preparation we use transparent rock crystal that is as free as possible from other substances. Pure quartz of this kind is used industrially for making lenses. If we take a magnifying glass, allow the Sun to shine through it and hold a paper underneath, it will catch fire and burn. The substance of silica and the way it is formed means that, like a lens, it can gather and strengthen the light and warmth effect.

We are of course not holding a lens over the plant when we use horn silica. In making the preparation we put the finely ground quartz into a cow horn. The horn's form and its spiralling tendency has a strong and concentrated effect within biological processes. It is placed into

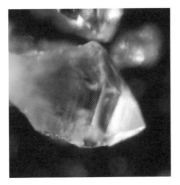

Quartz crystal (enlarged)   *Ground up 'silica sand' (enlarged)*

the earth for the whole summer, where it experiences the effect of the summer Sun and concentrates it in the preparation.

It is worth noting that Rudolf Steiner referred in his text to 'silica or quartz flour'. We must remember that in Steiner's day granules of flour were not as fine as today. In trials carried out by Maria Thun it was found that when quartz is ground as fine as flour is expected to be today, it is no longer capable of meeting the requirements of the preparation. The quality is reduced. The silica should not be ground so fine that it loses its crystalline structure. It would be better nowadays to therefore speak of fine silica sand.

We take a little less than ¼ oz (about 5 grams) of this preparation, stir it in an earthenware or wooden container for an hour in 10 to 13 gal (40–50 litres) and in doing so form good vortices. This is sufficient for an area of 2½ acres (1 ha).

Stirring should proceed from the perimeter of the container, intensifying towards the centre, and not from the centre outwards. By stirring in from the outside, layers of liquid rub against one another and draw in forces from the periphery. If we stir outward from the centre there is a dispersal and the effectiveness of the preparation is greatly reduced. The preparation's forces of light and warmth are transferred to the water.

Once stirring is completed the preparation must be sprayed within three or four hours. After that its effectiveness declines. On larger areas it is advisable to combine spraying with hoeing or harrowing; this saves a lot of time but also increases the effect of horn silica if the soil is simultaneously cultivated.

The effect on plants

Let us now return to the plant. We spray the preparation on the leaves of the plant. This seems to engender a change in the way the cells experience light. It is perhaps a kind of refraction such as we experience when, through a prism or in nature, the colors of the rainbow emerge. It appears that the differentiated effect of light on the plant calls forth a range of colors such as we often see in dew drops, which then stimulates the formation of various substances.

Depending on the cosmic influences active at the time the preparation is applied, the plant will then develop particular substances like proteins, fats, essential oils, sugars, salts or trace elements. If the light effect is too powerful the plant will not be able to cope with its intensity and cannot be creative. Something then occurs which may be compared to a certain level of burning that expresses itself in a hardening and regressive process in the plant.

For the practical application here is a brief overview:

- At *Root times* – potatoes, carrots, beetroot, etc. Spray applications in the morning during the early vigorous growth stages; later on, during the afternoon.
- At *Leaf times* – spinach, lettuce, kale, meadows, pastures, clover, etc. Spray applications in the morning or, if there is danger of bolting, in the afternoon.
- At *Flower times* – rape, buckwheat, mint, melissa, etc. Spray very early in the morning.
- At *Fruit times* – tomatoes, cucumbers, cereals, peas, beans, etc. Spray early in the morning.

Effects of the Moon at perigee and apogee
Titia Thun

The closest distance between the Moon and the Earth is called perigee (indicated by Pg), and the greatest distance is called apogee (Ag). Both have a major effect on plant growth. Perigee is always marked as a time to avoid and apogee stimulates flowering and fruiting. The almanac bars take this effect into account, overriding the underlying Moon/constellation effect.

Plants are influenced firstly by the constellation through which the Moon is passing and secondly by the movement of the Moon itself. The Moon follows an elliptical orbit which bring it closer or further away from the Earth. When it is closest to the Earth it expresses a downward pressing force on the plant. The plant is then focused entirely on its roots – one might say it is forced to its knees. In the trials carried out by Maria Thun it was found to have a strong growth-suppressing effect, which is why these times are marked as unfavourable. Seeds requiring light germinate badly when sown at this time. The plants are stunted, seem not to want to grow and increasingly have to struggle against pests and disease. Plants that are cultivated during perigee are more likely to produce infertile seeds.

This effect on the plant disappears as the Moon moves further from the Earth on its orbit.

The opposite tends to occur when the Moon reaches its apogee. As it moves further away from the Earth, it is as if the Moon draws the plant up with it. For seed producing plants this can be beneficial. However, most root or leaf plants respond negatively to being sown or cultivated during these times, with the exception of the potato.

What the Moon's apogee stimulates in the plant is not unlike that which occurs during Flower times. The plant tends to grow upwards and it responds in a similar but not identical way to a plant sown or cultivated when the Moon is in a Flower/Light constellation. Such a constellation has the effect of strengthening the plant so that it can develop strong, vibrant and long-lasting flowers. The roots and leaves are not repressed nor is seed formation, they are simply not supported by it. The flower is the object of a plant's upward growth.

For every plant, regardless of its specific focus, the root, leaf, flower and fruit are all important. Potatoes need foliage in order to grow, lettuce need a root, apple trees must flower and roses form hips. Even when growth is stimulated in a certain direction by a particular Moon constellation or a trine, there is still a harmonious relationship. The situation is different when the Moon is at its apogee, because at that time such harmony is not present. At these times the Moon takes an extreme position. It stretches out or constricts the plant in a one-sided way. This is not ideal for any plant. The effect of apogee is least harmful to flower and fruit formation.

For this reason the times of apogee are marked as Flower times in the almanac unless the constellation through which the Moon passing is already a Warmth/Fruit or Light/Flower constellation. The negative influence of apogee applies especially to the root and leaf and this is why cultivation of such plants should then be avoided. Due to the similarities to Light/Flower times the time of apogee is best utilized for cultivating flowering plants. For them any harm will be minimal. The best thing, however, and what is always recommended, is to cultivate flowers at true Flower times; that is when the Moon is in Gemini, Libra or Aquarius, or when there is a light trine. (Look out for the yellow constellation signs, ♊, ♎, ♒, or the yellow trine sign, ▲, at these times.) For activities focused specifically on enhancing the impulse of light as when working with oil producing plants, apogee can in no way replace a genuine Flower time.